A Concise Guide to Eighties' Music

KARL VORDERMAN

PARKBENCH PUBLICATIONS

Published in Great Britain by Parkbench Publications,
PO Box 1081, Belfast BT1 9EP

A CIP catalogue record for this title is available from the
British Library

ISBN 978-0-9555756-6-2

Designed and typeset by Bookcraft Ltd,
Stroud, Gloucestershire
Printed and bound in Great Britain by
CPI Antony Rowe, Eastbourne

CONTENTS

JUST WHO THE HELL IS
KARL VORDERMAN?

Born in a maternity hospital many years ago.
Tried to grow up.
Went to school and even university too.
Went off to work.
Left work and went off to new work.
Tried other work.
Got increasingly bored.
Started writing about popular music.
Went off to live in a little cottage at the edge of the woods.
Lived happily ever after.

If you have been disturbed and moved to tears by this sad tale of this remarkable loser, then perhaps you might want to make a donation. Please give generously to S.P.I.T.E (the Society for the Protection of Talented Enigmas), PO Box 1081, Belfast, BT1 9EP.

The song of the month for January 1980

Guns Of Navarone by The Specials (peak chart position:No.1)

The Specials can lay a credible claim to recording the most successful 'extended player' in British chart history, as their live E.P. (featuring 'Too Much Too Young') somersaulted to the top of the U.K. hit parade in early 1980. This mini-album contained five frantic interpretations of previous classic ska recordings from the likes of the Pioneers. However, my preference is for the hugely danceable 'Guns Of Navarone' which is a cover of an old Skatalites tune, which itself was borrowed from the epic movie of 1961. Here the veteran Anglo-Jamaican trombonist Rico Rodriguez blows up a storm. Is it possible to sit still to this energetic delight?

The song of the month for February 1980

Atomic by Blondie (peak chart position:No.1)

'Atomic' had been previously recorded almost a year ago for the 'Eat To The Beat' project. Remarkably it was the third selection for release as a single in Britain after 'Dreaming' had narrowly failed to reach Number One and 'Union City Blue' had mysteriously failed to reach the Top Ten. This awesome tune had no such misfortune. Co-written by the keyboardist Jimmy Destri, this four and a half minute treat benefited from an accompanying video which envisaged the group playing at a post-nuclear holocaust concert. The trademark interplay of guitars and Debbie Harry's vocals never sounded better. What a sensational start to the 1980s!

The song of the month for March 1980

King by UB40 (peak chart position: No.4)

'King' formed part of a double A-side with the equally popular 'Food For Thought' and became one of the great stories of the independent music labels' scene when this Graduate Records product climbed into the British Top Five in the spring of 1980. This tribute to Martin Luther King from a multi-racial Birmingham outfit had most peculiar origins. This strapped-for-cash reggae group had to record this seminal track at their producer Bob Lamb's bedsit, which also doubled up as a home-made recording studio. This home-made hit was the humble origin of a popular bunch who became a British musical institution in the ensuing three decades.

The song of the month for April 1980

A Forest by The Cure (peak chart position: No.31)

Goth-rockers The Cure were too much of a cult act to ever expect much commercial success in the singles chart. Having said that, this didn't deter them from releasing several 45s which were considerably better than their chart positions would indicate. Chief among them was the terrific 'A Forest'. This atmospheric number with the slightly sinister guitar sound narrowly failed to penetrate the British Top 30, but then it only succeeded in confirming that some songs are just too good for the charts. The mesmeric 'A Forest' was one such song.

The song of the month for May 1980

Best Friend by The Beat (peak chart position: No.22)

The Beat had previously hit the ground running when their debut single, a re-working of Smokey Robinson's 'Tears Of A Clown' reached the Top Ten at the turn of the year. The group then followed up with two more Top Ten forays courtesy of 'Hands Off ... She's Mine' and 'Mirror In The Bathroom'. Their fourth release was their least successful to date, and yet it was arguably the best. 'Best Friend' has to be one of the great jangly guitar songs of the 'eighties. It formed part of a double A-side with the overtly political 'Stand Down Margaret'. Both songs first surfaced when the excellent album 'I Just Can't Stop It' was issued in May.

The song of the month for June 1980

Love Will Tear Us Apart by Joy Division (peak chart position: No.13)

The appearance of 'Love Will Tear Us Apart' in the Top Twenty was bitter-sweet for Joy Division. Having just lost their lead vocalist Ian Curtis as a result of suicide, Manchester's finest new wave act were themselves effectively dead. Nevertheless, this posthumous single was a reminder of the soul-searching that afflicted the tormented psyche of Curtis. This poignant item was later bravely covered by Paul Young, but this original is just too good to imitate. The remaining members of the 'division' licked their considerable wounds from the tragic loss of Curtis and promptly re-appeared in the guise of the hugely respected New Order indie act.

The song of the month for July 1980

Private Life by Grace Jones (peak chart position: No.17)

Jamaican chanteuse Grace Jones staked an early claim for the best cover version of the decade when she expertly re-interpreted 'Private Life' which had originally saw the light of day on the Pretenders' debut album. With the notable assistance of Sly Dunbar and Robbie Shakespeare, Jones unleashes a reggae wonder. Chrissie Hynde's brutal lyrics were tailor-made for Jones whose deadpan delivery does justice to such put-downs as "You ask my advice/I say use the door/ But you're still clinging to somebody you deplore." "I just feel pity when you lie/Contempt when you cry." This insensitive item was included on the 'Warm Leatherette' long player.

The song of the month for August 1980

Biko by Peter Gabriel (peak chart position: No.38)

The great Peter Gabriel was the latest artist to exploit the medium of popular music as an outlet for political protest. The ex-Genesis vocalist commendably decided to share his profound misgivings about the circumstances surrounding the death of Steve Biko with the rest of the world via this landmark recording. Gabriel recruited African vocalists as well as Phil Collins and even made use of bagpipes on this remarkable single. Gabriel's revulsion at apartheid is best summed in the following extract:"You can blow out a candle/ But you can't blow out a fire/ Once the flame begins to catch/ The wind will blow it higher." Superb stuff.

The song of the month for September 1980

Three Little Birds by Bob Marley & The Wailers
(peak chart position: No.17)

Marley's classic 'Three Little Birds' had originally been hatched three years earlier when it appeared on the popular 'Exodus' album. Eventually Island Records decided to issue it as a single. The simple but effective lyrics were uplifting for all who had the good fortune to hear it: "Don't worry about a thing/Cos every little thing is gonna be all right." Ironically, while this fine reggae pop song was climbing the British hit parade, the great man himself collapsed in Central Park in New York whilst jogging. Inoperable cancer was soon diagnosed and Marley then fought a losing battle against terminal illness for the last seven months of his life.

The song of the month for October 1980

Woman In Love by Barbra Streisand (peak chart position: No.1)

Barbra Streisand had previously flirted with the top regions of the charts with her collaborations with Neil Diamond and then Donna Summer. However, the Jewess decided that 'enough is enough' and she proceeded to treat the airwaves to a new solo recording, 'Woman In Love'. This romantic celebration certainly found favour with record buyers on both sides of the Atlantic Ocean as it became a deserved chart-topper. The song would also prove to be one of the biggest-sellers of 1980.

The song of the month for November 1980

(Just Like) Starting Over by John Lennon (peak chart position: No.1)

John Lennon had gone into a self-imposed retreat from stardom and from recording music from early 1975 through to the summer of 1980 when he eventually swapped his house-husband duties for his more familiar role of a performing artist. The Beatle legend soon delivered a new album in collaboration with his less musically gifted wife, thus yielding the 'Double Fantasy' project. One highlight of this long player was the admirable rocker in which John states "It'll be just like starting over." However, it proved to be a false start as the author of some of the world's best love and peace anthems was gunned down in early December.

The song of the month for December 1980

The Call Up by The Clash (peak chart position: No.40)

The Clash were faced with the unenviable task of attempting to improve upon the critically acclaimed 'London Calling' double album. They not surprisingly failed, although they did themselves no favours by lumping all their new material together onto a triple album, entitled 'Sandinista'. Nevertheless, this newly-released long player did have a number of highlights, including 'Somebody Got Murdered' and 'Bankrobber'. My own preference is for the anti-draft track, 'The Call Up'. This item features a wailing klaxon acting as a call to arms. What may have confused some observers was that the seemingly belligerent Clash were actually pacifists!

THE TOP 10 BEST SELLING UK SINGLES OF 1980

1 Don't Stand So Close To Me by The Police

2 Woman In Love by Barbra Streisand

3 Feels Like I'm In Love by Kelly Marie

4 Super Trouper by Abba

5 D.I.S.C.O. by Ottawan

6 The Tide Is High by Blondie

7 Geno by Dexy's Midnight Runners

8 Coward Of The County by Kenny Rogers

9 Together We Are Beautiful by Fern Kinney

10 (Just Like) Starting Over by John Lennon

ALBUM OF THE YEAR FOR 1980

Remain In Light by Talking Heads (released in October)

Side 1

1. Born Under Punches
   (The Heat Goes On); 5:46

2. Crosseyed and Painless; 4:45

3. The Great Curve; 6:26

Side 2

1. Once In A Lifetime; 4:19

2. Houses In Motion; 4:30

3. Seen And Not Seen; 3:20

4. Listening Wind; 4:42

5. The Overload; 6:00

I think that I have about fourteen studio albums from 1980 in my possession, so this is clearly my favourite year in the history of popular music. I have a marginal preference for 'Remain In Light' which perhaps represents the creative peak of the extremely creative and quirky quartet, Talking Heads. I have often regarded these New Yorkers as the Pink Floyd of punk, in that they were always a bit more arty and cleverer than their peers and contemporaries. This bizarre album is a case in point. It features new ethnic sounds and rhythms before 'world music' was championed by the likes of Peter Gabriel and Paul Simon. The project also showcases the production talents of Brian Eno (a refugee from Roxy Music). 'Once In A Lifetime' made a deserved splash in the singles charts, but it is eclipsed by the excellent 'Houses In Motion'. 'Seen And Not Seen' is another highlight, but pride of place goes to the energetic opener which descends into the refrain: "Goes on/And the heat goes on/ Goes on/And the heat goes on." Chart material it wasn't. Compulsive listening it was.

THE UK NUMBER ONE ALBUMS
OF 1980

12 Jan: Abba – Greatest Hits Volume 2;	1 week
19 Jan: The Pretenders – Pretenders;	4 weeks
16 Feb: Various artist comp. (Motown) – The Last Dance;	2 weeks
01 Mar: The Shadows – String Of Hits;	3 weeks
22 Mar: Johnny Mathis – Tears And Laughter;	2 weeks
05 Apr: Genesis – Duke;	2 weeks
19 Apr: Rose Royce – Greatest Hits;	2 weeks
03 May: Sky – Sky 2;	2 weeks
17 May: Boney M – The Magic Of Boney M;	2 weeks
31 May: Paul McCartney – McCartney II;	2 weeks
14 Jun: Peter Gabriel – Peter Gabriel;	2 weeks
28 Jun: Roxy Music – Flesh And Blood;	1 week
05 Jul: The Rolling Stones – Emotional Rescue;	2 weeks
19 Jul: Queen – The Game;	2 weeks
02 Aug: Deep Purple – Deepest Purple;	1 week
09 Aug: AC/DC – Back In Black;	2 weeks
23 Aug: Roxy Music – Flesh And Blood;	3 weeks
13 Sep: Gary Numan – Telekon;	1 week
20 Sep: Kate Bush – Never For Ever;	1 week
27 Sep: David Bowie – Scary Monsters And Super Creeps;	2 weeks
11 Oct: The Police – Zenyatta Mondatta;	4 weeks
08 Nov: Barbra Streisand – Guilty;	2 weeks
22 Nov: Abba – Super Trouper;	9 weeks

THE US NUMBER ONE ALBUMS
OF 1980

05 Jan: Donna Summer – On The Radio;   1 week

12 Jan: The Bee Gees – Bee Gees Greatest;   1 week

19 Jan: Pink Floyd – The Wall;   15 weeks

03 May: Bob Seger & The Silver Bullet Band – Against The Wind;   6 weeks

14 Jun: Billy Joel – Glass Houses;   6 weeks

26 Jul: The Rolling Stones – Emotional Rescue;   7 weeks

13 Sep: Jackson Browne – Hold Out;   1 week

20 Sep: Queen – The Game: 5 weeks

25 Oct: Barbra Streisand – Guilty;   2 weeks

08 Nov: Bruce Springsteen – The River;   4 weeks

06 Dec: Barbra Streisand – Guilty;   1 week

13 Dec: Kenny Rogers – Greatest Hits;   2 week

27 Dec: John Lennon And Yoko Ono – Double Fantasy

THE UK NUMBER ONE SINGLES OF 1980

19 Jan: The Pretenders – Brass In Pocket;   2 weeks

02 Feb: The Special AKA (Specials) – The Specials Live EP;   2 weeks

16 Feb: Kenny Rogers – Coward Of The County;   2 weeks

01 Mar: Blondie – Atomic;   2 weeks

15 Mar: Fern Kinney – Together We Are Beautiful;   1 week

22 Mar: The Jam – Going Underground/Dreams Of Children;   3 weeks

12 Apr: The Detroit Spinners – Working My Way Back To You;   2 weeks

26 Apr: Blondie – Call Me;   1 week

03 May: Dexy's Midnight Runners – Geno;   2 weeks

17 May: Johnny Logan – What's Another Year;   2 weeks

31 May: Mash – Suicide Is Painless (Theme from M*A*S*H);   3 weeks

21 Jun: Don McLean – Crying;   3 weeks

12 Jul: Olivia Newton-John & Electric Light Orchestra – Xanadu;   2 weeks

26 Jul: Odyssey – Use It Up And Wear It Out;   2 weeks

09 Aug: Abba – The Winner Takes It All;   2 weeks

23 Aug: David Bowie – Ashes To Ashes;   2 weeks

06 Sep: The Jam – Start;   1 week

13 Sep: Kelly Marie – Feels Like I'm In Love;   2 weeks

27 Sep: The Police – Don't Stand So Close To Me;   4 weeks

25 Oct: Barbra Streisand – Woman In Love;   3 weeks

15 Nov: Blondie – The Tide Is High;   2 weeks

29 Nov: Abba – Super Trouper;   3 weeks

20 Dec: John Lennon – (Just Like) Starting Over;   1 week

27 Dec: St Winifred's School Choir – There's No One Quite Like Grandma;   2 weeks

THE US NUMBER ONE SINGLES OF 1980

05 Jan: KC And The Sunshine Band – Please Don't Go;	1 week
12 Jan: Rupert Holmes – Escape (The Pina Colada Song);	1 week
19 Jan: Michael Jackson – Rock With You;	4 weeks
16 Feb: Captain & Tennille – Do That To Me One More Time;	1 week
23 Feb: Queen – Crazy Little Thing Called Love;	4 weeks
22 Mar: Pink Floyd – Another Brick In The Wall (Part II);	4 weeks
19 Apr: Blondie – Call Me;	6 weeks
31 May: Lipps Inc – Funkytown;	4 weeks
28 Jun: Paul McCartney – Coming Up (Live At Glasgow);	3 weeks
19 Jul: Billy Joel – It's Still Rock And Roll To Me;	2 weeks
02 Aug: Olivia Newton-John – Magic;	4 weeks
30 Aug: Christopher Cross – Sailing;	1 week
06 Sep: Diana Ross – Upside Down;	4 weeks
04 Oct: Queen – Another One Bites The Dust;	3 weeks
25 Oct: Barbra Streisand – Woman In Love;	3 weeks
15 Nov: Kenny Rogers – Lady;	6 weeks
27 Dec: John Lennon – (Just Like) Starting Over	

THE 'UNSUCCESSFUL' UK NUMBER TWO SINGLES OF 1980

19 Jan: Billy Preston & Syreeta – With You I'm Born Again;   2 weeks

23 Feb: The Whispers – And The Beat Goes On;   1 week

05 Apr: Liquid Gold – Dance Yourself Dizzy;   2 weeks

03 May: Paul McCartney – Coming Up;   1 week

24 May: Hot Chocolate – No Doubt About It;   3 weeks

28 Jun: Lipps Inc – Funkytown;   2 weeks

02 Aug: Leo Sayer – More Than I Can Say;   1 week

09 Aug: Diana Ross – Upside Down;   2 weeks

20 Sep: Randy Crawford – One Day I'll Fly Away;   2 weeks

04 Oct: Stevie Wonder – Masterblaster (Jammin');   1 week

11 Oct: Ottawan – D.I.S.C.O.;   3 weeks

01 Nov: Status Quo – What You're Proposing;   2 weeks

THE 'UNSUCCESSFUL' US NUMBER TWO SINGLES OF 1980

01 Mar: Teri DeSario And KC – Yes I'm Ready

15 Mar: Dan Fogelberg – Longer

29 Mar: The Detroit Spinners – Working My Way Back To You

26 Apr: Christopher Cross – Ride Like The Wind

13 Sep: Air Supply – All Out Of Love

06 Dec: Leo Sayer – More Than I Can Say

NEWS HIGHLIGHTS OF 1980

January 2nd: The first steel strike since 1926 begins in Britain.

January 13th: Joshua Nkomo returns to Zimbabwe-Rhodesia after three year's exile.

January 27th: Robert Mugabe returns to Zimbabwe-Rhodesia after five year's exile.

February 12th: The Winter Olympics open at Lake Placid, near New York.

February 18th: Pierre Trudeau returns to power in Canada's general election.

February 27th: A general election begins in Zimbabwe-Rhodesia.

March 4th: Robert Mugabe is elected as Zimbabwe's first black Prime Minister.

March 16th: Alan Minter becomes world middleweight boxing champion.

March 23rd: The deposed Shah of Iran flees Panama for Cairo.

April 18th: Zimbabwe achieves independence, ending British rule in Africa.

April 25th: An American attempt to rescue their hostages goes horribly wrong.

April 30th: Three gunmen seize hostages at the Iranian embassy in London.

May 1st: Ian MacGregor is appointed chairman of the British Steel Corporation.

May 5th: The SAS successfully storm the besieged Iranian embassy in London.

May 19th: North America's Mount St. Helens experiences a volcanic eruption.

June 12th: British Steel announces the September closure of its Consett works.

June 12th: England football fans riot at a Turin European Championship match.

June 16th: Police and blacks clash at an anniversary of Soweto's revolt.

July 10th: A huge fire damages north London's Alexandra Palace.

July 16th: Ronald Reagan is nominated as the Republicans' Presidential candidate.

July 19th: President Brezhnev opens the Olympic Games in Moscow.

August 14th: Jimmy Carter wins the Democrats' nomination for the November election.

August 27th: Steve Ovett sets a new 1500 metres world record.

August 27th: New figures reveal Britain's unemployment total is now two million.

September 11th: A Chilean referendum approves an extension to Pinochet's rule.

September 24th: Saddam Hussein's Iraqi troops invade Iran.

September 27th: Alan Minter loses his world boxing crown to Marvin Hagler.

October 10th: Mrs Thatcher tells the Conservatives she is "not for turning".

October 15th: James Callaghan resigns as the British Labour Party leader.

October 17th: The Queen makes an historic state visit to the Vatican.

November 4th: Ronald Reagan trounces Jimmy Carter to become President.

November 10th: Michael Foot narrowly defeats Denis Healey to become Labour leader.

November 13th: Denis Healey is elected as the Labour Party deputy leader.

December 12th: An IRA hunger strike at the Maze Prison is abandoned.

December 14th: Thousands observe a vigil for the departed John Lennon.

December 18th: Three dangerous criminals escape from London's Brixton Prison.

SPORT IN 1980

English Division One football champions: Liverpool; runners-up: Manchester United

English FA Cup final: West Ham United 1 Arsenal 0

English League Cup Final: Wolverhampton Wanderers 1 Nottingham Forest 0

Scottish Premier League football champions: Aberdeen; runners-up: Glasgow Celtic

Scottish FA Cup final: Glasgow Celtic 1 Glasgow Rangers 0 (after extra time)

Scottish League Cup final: Dundee United 3 Aberdeen 0 (in a replay)

Irish League football champions: Linfield; Irish Cup final: Linfield 2 Crusaders 0

League Of Ireland football champions: Limerick; cup winners: Waterford United

European Cup final: Nottingham Forest 1 Hamburg 0

European Cup-Winners' Cup final: Valencia beat Arsenal 5–4 on penalties

UEFA Cup final: Eintracht Frankfurt beat Borussia Monchengladbach on away goals rule

English county cricket champions: Middlesex

Five Nations' rugby union champions: England (the 'grand slam')

Formula One world drivers' champion: Alan Jones (Australia) in a Williams car

Gaelic football All-Ireland champions: Kerry; runners-up: Roscommon

British Open golf champion: Tom Watson (at Muirfield)

US Masters golf champion: Seve Ballesteros

US Open golf champion: Jack Nicklaus

USPGA golf champion: Jack Nicklaus

Rugby league Challenge Cup final: Hull Kingston Rovers 10 Hull 5

Wimbledon men's singles tennis final: B Borg beat J McEnroe 1–6, 7–5, 6–3, 6–7, 8–6

Wimbledon ladies' singles tennis final: E Cawley beat C Evert 6–1, 7–6

World snooker final: Cliff Thorburn (Canada) beat Alex Higgins (Northern Ireland) 18–16

The Aintree Grand National steeplechase winner: Ben Nevis; price 40–1

The Epsom Derby winner: Henbit; jockey – Willie Carson; price 7–1

European Championship final: West Germany 2 Belgium 1 (in Rome)

1980's BUCKET-KICKERS

January 3rd: Joy Adamson (British naturalist); aged 59

January 18th: Sir Cecil Walter Hardy Beaton (British photographer); aged 76

January 29th: Jimmy Durante (US comedian); aged 86

February 17th: Graham Sutherland (British artist); aged 76

February 22nd: Oskar Kokoschka (Austrian artist); aged 93

March 10th: Dr Herman Tarnower (US author); aged 69

March 26th: Roland Barthes (French philosopher); aged 64

March 31st: Jesse Owens (US athlete); aged 66

April 15th: Jean-Paul Sartre (French philosopher); aged 74

April 29th: Sir Alfred Joseph Hitchcock (British director); aged 80

May 4th: Marshal Tito (Yugoslav President); aged 87

May 18th: Ian Kevin Curtis (British singer); aged 23

June 7th: Philip Guston (US artist); aged 66

June 7th: Henry Miller (US writer); aged 89

June 12th: Sir William Butlin (British businessman); aged 80

June 23rd: Sanjay Gandhi (Indian politician); aged 33

July 13th: Sir Seretse Khama (Botswana's President); aged 59

July 24th: Richard Henry Peter Sellers (British comedian); aged 54

July 27th: Shah Mohammed Reza Pahlavi (ex-Iranian monarch); aged 60

September 17th: Anastasio Somoza Debayle (ex-Nicaraguan dictator); aged 54

September 25th: John Bonham (British musician); aged 32

November 4th: Johnny Owen (British boxer); aged 24

November 7th: Steve McQueen (US actor); aged 50

November 9th: Patrick Gordon Campbell (Irish journalist); aged 67

November 22nd: Mae West (US actress); aged 88

December 3rd: Sir Oswald Mosley (British politician); aged 84

December 8th: John Ono Lennon (British musician); aged 40

December 18th: Alexei Kosygin (Soviet statesman); aged 76

December 24th: Grand Admiral Karl Doenitz (German commander); aged 89

The song of the month for January 1981

Vienna by Ultravox (peak chart position: No.2)

The British record-buying public have been known to let themselves down on a number of occasions. One such notable instance was when they allowed the rather silly novelty song 'Shaddap Your Face' to occupy the Number One position ahead of the magnificent 'Vienna'. Dear oh dear. It is actually quite ironic but 'Vienna' actually sold more copies than the masterpiece from the Joe Dolce Music Theatre. Anyhow, this is unquestionably Ultravox's finest track and it is a strong candidate for the accolade of best song of 1981, although it was actually recorded the previous year. Its black and white video is as memorable as the song itself.

The song of the month for February 1981

Jealous Guy by Roxy Music (peak chart position: No.1)

The tragic death of John Lennon not surprisingly prompted the release of much of his esteemed material into the public domain as record companies and other artists both cashed in on his death and paid their own unique tribute. For example, George Harrison stepped forth with the admirable 'All Those Years Ago', Elton John released 'I Saw Her Standing There', Phil Collins recorded a formidable version of 'Tomorrow Never Knows' and Roxy Music finally made it to the top of the hit parade with their re-working of a song that had first surfaced on the 'Imagine' album. To be fair to Roxy Music, their own effort improves on Lennon's solo original.

The song of the month for March 1981

Just A Feeling by Bad Manners (peak chart position: No.13)

Maybe it's just a feeling on my part, but the crazy bunch of Bad Manners never received the kudos that they perhaps merited. 'Just A Feeling' narrowly missed out on the British Top Ten, which is regrettable given the terrific harmonica of Winston Bazoomies. Bad Manners with their cartoon frontman, Buster Bloodvessel, were responsible for many oddball tunes which are nothing if not interesting. This fine single was a product of the aptly-titled 'Loonee Tunes' album, which also contained such gems as the hit single 'Lorraine', 'El Pussycat', and the energetic 'Undersea Adventures Of Ivor The Engine.' Now that's what I call a bit of culture.

The song of the month for April 1981

Flowers Of Romance by Public Image Limited (peak chart position: No. 24)

Don't be fooled by the song title folks. There was nothing remotely floral or romantic about this John Lydon composition. The punk legend was enjoying a new lease of life, free from the manoeuvrings of the dastardly Malcolm McLaren, and with Public Image Limited he now had the opportunity to express his own art and individuality. 'Flowers Of Romance' is short and to the point. It builds with an awesome drum-beat before young Johnny unleashes his cynicism:"I can't depend on these so-called friends." The tune sounds a bit sinister, revealing John's wicked sense of humour and it certainly stood out from all the other songs in the Top 40.

The song of the month for May 1981

One Day In Your Life by Michael Jackson (peak chart position: No.1)

Michael Jackson had previously visited the top of the British singles lists in collabora-tion with the rest of his family on the dancefloor classic 'Show You The Way To Go'. The former infant prodigy subsequently decided that the way to go was on his own, away from any family assistance. It was slightly ironic that whilst Jackson had enjoyed new critical acclaim and increased record sales with the tremendous 'Off The Wall' album of 1979, the song which propelled him to the summit of the British charts had been recorded long before 'Off The Wall'. 'One Day In Your Life' is a beautiful item, and only a heart of stone could fail to agree.

The song of the month for June 1981

Friday Night, Saturday Morning by The Specials (peak chart position: No.1)

It's seems rather strange that the hugely popular Specials should choose to go their separate ways at the very time when they ought to have been dining out on the glory of their most successful single, 'Ghost Town'. Unfortunately group disharmony decreed that this would be the last outing for Coventry's finest septet. It probably seems rather sacrilegious of me but I have a preference for the flip side of 'Ghost Town'. Here one finds Lynval Golding's 'Why' which addresses a recent racist knife attack on him. However, I am especially keen on 'Friday Night, Saturday Morning'. Terry Hall's travails about a night on the pull are most amusing.

The song of the month for July 1981

Girls On Film by Duran Duran (peak chart position: No.5)

With the demise of Two Tone and British ska, a new fad stepped into the vacuum. It was now the turn of the New Romantics with their synthesizers and their melodrama to capture the attention of the teenage market. Birmingham's Duran Duran were certainly bedroom poster material, but they were also responsible for many great singles. After 'Planet Earth' had introduced them to the music industry, the group really found their feet with the admirable 'Girls On Film'. Critics may have scoffed at what they perceived as escapist, make believe nonsense, but Duran Duran and their glamorous videos certainly struck a chord with Britain's 'yoof'.

The song of the month for August 1981

Day After Day by The Pretenders (peak chart position: No.45)

Day After Day was the least successful of the four tracks issued from the Pretenders' second album, yet it is arguably the most impressive. It took me a while to warm to this tune, but its piano and the heavier guitar sound distinguishes it from the rest of the group's jangly guitar repertoire. This was one of the last occasions when music enthusiasts would have the opportunity to acquaint themselves with the product of a band that soon descended into turmoil in June 1982 when bass player Pete Farndon was sacked for excessive drug use literally days before the talented guitarist James Honeyman-Scott died from a drugs overdose.

The song of the month for September 1981

Prince Charming by Adam And The Ants (peak chart position: No.1)

How appropriate that the flamboyant Adam Ant should sing that "ridicule is nothing to be scared of". In 1981, Adam and his insects, having fled from their punk origins, were the flavour of the month, for just about every month. Previously 'Stand And Deliver' with its amusing tale of a highwayman (no laughing matter for his victims) had climbed to the top of the British charts, and the Ant colony colonised the pop summit again in the autumn with another large dollop of tongue-in-cheek lyrics. 'Prince Charming' was indeed a charmer of a single, but hereafter vocalist Stuart Goddard would slowly slide from fame into the oblivion of depression.

The song of the month for October 1981

Every Little Thing She Does Is Magic by The Police
(peak chart position: No.1)

I must confess to being more lukewarm than most to the 'great' Police. However, 'Every Little Thing' was a deserved chart-topper. This particular love song was a far cry from a previous one of twelve months earlier when 'Don't Stand So Close To Me' was a tale of a schoolgirl crush. More recently, the Police had dipped their toes in the stormy waters of political controversy with the outstanding 'Invisible Sun', but this time the trio abandoned the armalite in favour of the more conventional formula of a romantic tune. Sting's lyrics are unashamedly a celebration of being in love. There were clearly enough record-buyers who empathised.

The song of the month for November 1981

Under Pressure by Queen And David Bowie (peak chart position: No.1)

It was only to be expected that two of the great heavyweight acts of the previous decade should deliver an item of pure class. This song kicks off with that memorable John Deacon bass line, 'borrowed' thereafter by the likes of Vanilla Ice on 'Ice Ice Baby'. However, here is one occasion when neither Queen nor Bowie were under any pressure. The Fab Four were after all basking in the growing triumph of their 'Greatest Hits' album which went on to reside in the album charts for several years. I do so like the Bowie line about "Keep coming up with love/When it's so slashed and torn." They just don't make them like this anymore.

The song of the month for December 1981

Don't You Want Me? by The Human League (peak chart position: No.1)

The Yuletide season had become notorious for attracting a plethora of novelty acts who made logic-defying progress up to the top of the charts. Such formidable rock acts as Clive Dunn, Benny Hill, St.Winifred's School Choir, and Little Jimmy Osmond had all been there and done that. It was therefore something of a pleasant surprise when Sheffield's Human League helped themselves to an unlikely Christmas chart-topper with the far from merry 'Don't You Want Me'. The song benefits from trademark synthesizers as well as an interesting story. Phil Oakley might no longer have been 'wanted' but his song was wanted in large quantities.

THE TOP 10 BEST SELLING UK SINGLES OF 1981

1 Tainted Love by Soft Cell
2 Stand And Deliver by Adam & The Ants
3 Prince Charming by Adam & The Ants
4 This Ole House by Shakin' Stevens
5 Vienna by Ultravox
6 Making Your Mind Up by Bucks Fizz
7 One Day In Your Life by Michael Jackson
8 Shaddup You Face by Joe Dolce Music Theatre
9 Birdie Song by The Tweets
10 You Drive Me Crazy by Shakin' Stevens

ALBUM OF THE YEAR FOR 1981:
Celebrate The Bullet by The Selecter (released in February)

Side 1:

1. (Who Likes) Facing Situations; 3:32
2. Deep Water; 4:09
3. Red Reflections; 3:38
4. Tell Me What's Wrong; 4:30
5. Bombscare; 3:05
6. Washed Up and Left For Dead; 3:57

Side 2:

1. Celebrate The Bullet; 4:34
2. Selling Out Your Future; 3:59
3. Cool Blue Lady; 3:30
4. Their Dream Goes On; 3:42
5. Bristol And Miami; 4:58

Some albums can be something of an anti-climax because by the time that they are released, you are already familiar with a few of the ten items, which have previously been issued as singles. 'Celebrate The Bullet' therefore is something of a luxury as the eleven previously unheard tracks are still waiting to be discovered. Whilst many subsequent records profited from exposure on MTV as well as advertising campaigns conducted like a military offensive, this album had no such assistance. Having exited the Two Tone record label, the Selecter attempted to travel away from their high-energy ska origins into something more sophisticated, yet still danceable. The group commendably relied on their own material, with songwriting credits shared amongst a few of the members. The long player draws to an epic conclusion with 'Bristol And Miami' which recalls the race riots in those two locations in 1980. This record was subsequently washed up and left for dead as the musical climate changed, but here is one occasion when a lack of album sales was a great injustice.

THE UK NUMBER ONE ALBUMS
OF 1981

24 Jan: Adam & The Ants – Kings Of The Wild Frontier;		2 weeks
07 Feb: John Lennon & Yoko Ono – Double Fantasy;		2 weeks
21 Feb: Phil Collins – Face Value;		3 weeks
14 Mar: Adam & The Ants – Kings Of The Wild Frontier;		10 weeks
23 May: Star Sound – Stars On 45;		5 weeks
27 Jun: Motorhead – No Sleep Till Hammersmith;		1 week
04 Jul: Various artist comp. (Ronco) – Disco Daze And Disco Nites;		1 week
11 Jul: Cliff Richard – Love Songs;		5 weeks
15 Aug: Various artist comp. – Official BBC Album Of The Royal Wedding;		2 weeks
29 Aug: Electric Light Orchestra – Time;		2 weeks
12 Sep: Meat Loaf – Dead Ringer;		2 weeks
26 Sep: Genesis – Abacab;		2 weeks
10 Oct: The Police – Ghost In The Machine;		3 weeks
31 Oct: Human League – Dare!;		1 week
07 Nov: Shakin' Stevens – Shaky;		1 week
14 Nov: Queen – Queen's Greatest Hits;		4 weeks
12 Dec: Various artist comp. (K-Tel) – Chart Hits '81;		1 week
19 Dec: Abba – The Visitors;		3 weeks

THE US NUMBER ONE ALBUMS OF 1981

03 Jan: John Lennon And Yoko Ono – Double Fantasy;	7 weeks
21 Feb: REO Speedwagon – Hi Infidelity;	6 weeks
04 Apr: Styx – Paradise Theater;	2 weeks
18 Apr: REO Speedwagon – Hi Infidelity;	3 weeks
09 May: Styx – Paradise Theater;	1 week
16 May: REO Speedwagon – Hi Infidelity;	6 weeks
27 Jun: Kim Carnes – Mistaken Identity;	4 weeks
25 Jul: The Moody Blues – Long Distance Voyager;	3 weeks
15 Aug: Pat Benatar – Precious Time;	1 week
22 Aug: Foreigner – 4;	2 weeks
05 Sep: Stevie Nicks – Bella Donna;	1 week
12 Sep: Journey – Escape;	1 week
19 Sep: The Rolling Stones – Tattoo You;	9 weeks
21 Nov: Foreigner – 4;	5 weeks
26 Dec: AC/DC – For Those About To Rock We Salute You	

THE UK NUMBER ONE SINGLES
OF 1981

10 Jan: John Lennon – Imagine;	4 weeks
07 Feb: John Lennon – Woman;	2 weeks
21 Feb: Joe Dolce Music Theatre – Shaddap You Face;	3 weeks
14 Mar: Roxy Music – Jealous Guy;	2 weeks
28 Mar: Shakin' Stevens – This Ole House;	3 weeks
18 Apr: Bucks Fizz – Making Your Mind Up;	3 weeks
09 May: Adam & The Ants – Stand And Deliver;	5 weeks
13 Jun: Smokey Robinson – Being With You;	2 weeks
27 Jun: Michael Jackson – One Day In Your Life;	2 weeks
11 Jul: The Specials – Ghost Town;	3 weeks
01 Aug: Shakin' Stevens – Green Door;	4 weeks
29 Aug: Aneka – Japanese Boy;	1 week
05 Sep: Soft Cell – Tainted Love;	2 weeks
19 Sep: Adam & The Ants – Prince Charming;	4 weeks
17 Oct: Dave Stewart & Barbara Gaskin – It's My Party;	4 weeks
14 Nov: The Police – Every Little Thing She Does Is Magic;	1 week
21 Nov: Queen & David Bowie – Under Pressure;	2 weeks
05 Dec: Julio Iglesias – Begin The Beguine (Volver A Empezar);	1 week
12 Dec: Human League – Don't You Want Me;	5 weeks

THE US NUMBER ONE SINGLES OF 1981

03 Jan: John Lennon – (Just Like) Starting Over;		4 weeks
31 Jan: Blondie – The Tide Is High;		1 week
07 Feb: Kool & The Gang – Celebration;		2 weeks
21 Feb: Dolly Parton – 9 To 5;		1 week
28 Feb: Eddie Rabbitt – I Love A Rainy Night;		2 weeks
14 Mar: Dolly Parton – 9 To 5;		1 week
21 Mar: REO Speedwagon – Keep On Loving You;		1 week
28 Mar: Blondie – Rapture;		2 weeks
11 Apr: Daryl Hall And John Oates – Kiss On My List;		3 weeks
02 May: Sheena Easton – Morning Train (Nine To Five);		2 weeks
16 May: Kim Carnes – Bette Davis Eyes;		5 weeks
20 Jun: Stars On 45 – Stars On 45 Medley;		1 week
27 Jun: Kim Carnes – Bette Davis Eyes;		4 weeks
25 Jul: Air Supply – The One That You Love;		1 week
01 Aug: Rick Springfield – Jessie's Girl;		2 weeks
15 Aug: Diana Ross & Lionel Richie – Endless Love;		9 weeks
17 Oct: Christopher Cross – Arthur's Theme (Best That You Can Do);		3 weeks
07 Nov: Daryl Hall And John Oates – Private Eyes;		2 weeks
21 Nov: Olivia Newton-John – Physical;		6 weeks

THE 'UNSUCCESSFUL' UK NUMBER
TWO SINGLES OF 1981

10 Jan: John & Yoko & The Plastic Ono Band – Happy Xmas (War Is Over); 1 week

17 Jan: Adam And The Ants – Ant Music;   2 weeks

07 Feb: Phil Collins – In The Air Tonight;   1 week

14 Feb: Ultravox – Vienna;   4 weeks

14 Mar: Adam And The Ants – Kings Of The Wild Frontier;   1 week

28 Mar: Kim Wilde – Kids In America;   2 weeks

25 Apr: Ennio Morricone – Chi Mai;   2 weeks

09 May: Starsound – Stars On 45;   1 week

16 May: Shakin' Stevens – You Drive Me Crazy;   4 weeks

13 Jun: Kate Robbins – More Than In Love;   1 week

18 July: Starsound – Stars On 45, II;   2 weeks

08 Aug: Stevie Wonder – Happy Birthday;   1 week

15 Aug: Royal Philharmonic Orchestra – Hooked On Classics;   2 weeks

03 Oct: The Police – Invisible Sun;   1 week

10 Oct: The Tweets – The Birdie Song;   2 weeks

24 Oct: Laurie Anderson – O Superman;   1 week

31 Oct: Altered Images – Happy Birthday;   3 weeks

12 Dec: Cliff Richard – Daddy's Home;   4 weeks

THE 'UNSUCCESSFUL' US NUMBER TWO SINGLES OF 1981

10 Jan: Neil Diamond – Love On The Rocks

21 Mar: John Lennon – Woman

02 May: Grover Washington Junior – Just The Two Of Us

23 May: Smokey Robinson – Being With You

04 Jul: George Harrison – All Those Years Ago

15 Aug: Joey Scarbury – Theme From The Greatest American Hero

29 Aug: The Pointer Sisters – Slow Hand

19 Sep: Juice Newton – Queen Of Hearts

31 Oct: The Rolling Stones – Start Me Up

28 Nov: Foreigner – Waiting For A Girl Like You

NEWS HIGHLIGHTS OF 1981

January 4th: Police arrest a man suspected of being the 'Yorkshire Ripper.'

January 21st: Iran releases its fifty-two American hostages.

January 25th: Four Labour Party right-wingers issue the Limehouse Declaration.

February 14th: 49 die in a fire at a Dublin disco.

February 23rd: Prince Charles is reportedly engaged to Lady Diana Spencer.

February 23rd: Soldiers burst into Spain's parliament in an attempted coup.

March 1st: Bobby Sands begins a hunger strike in the Maze Prison.

March 29th: The first-ever London Marathon is held.

March 30th: Ronald Reagan narrowly survives an assassination attempt.

April 3rd: Rioting occurs in Brixton and Southall.

April 11th: Bobby Sands wins the Fermanagh and South Tyrone by-election.

April 29th: Peter Sutcliffe confesses to being the Yorkshire Ripper.

May 8th: Ken Livingstone is elected leader of the Greater London Council.

May 10th: Francois Mitterand is elected as the new President of France.

May 13th: Pope John Paul II narrowly survives an assassination attempt.

June 21st: The Socialists win France's National Assembly general election.

June 30th: Shots are fired at the Queen during Trooping The Colour.

June 30th: Garret Fitzgerald succeeds Charles Haughey as the Irish Taoiseach.

July 5th: Rioting erupts in the Toxteth area of Liverpool.

July 21st: Willis bowls England to an unlikely Ashes victory at Headingley.

July 29th: Prince Charles marries Lady Diana Spencer in St. Paul's Cathedral.

August 2nd: Botham bowls England to another sensational Ashes win at Edgbaston.

August 24th: Mark Chapman is jailed for life for murdering John Lennon.

August 28th: Seb Coe breaks the world mile record in Brussels.

September 18th: David Steel tells the Liberals to "prepare for government."

September 18th: The guillotine is abolished in France.

September 27th: Tony Benn's attempt to become Labour's deputy leader is foiled.

October 3rd: The Maze Prison hunger strike ends, after ten deaths.

October 14th: Scotland qualify for the 1982 football World Cup in Spain.

October 24th: A huge anti-nuclear rally is held at Hyde Park.

November 10th: Hosni Mubarak is appointed as Egypt's new President.

November 18th: England and Northern Ireland qualify for the World Cup finals.

November 26th: Shirley Williams wins the Crosby by-election.

December 8th: Arthur Scargill becomes president of the National Union of Mineworkers.

December 13th: General Jaruzelski introduces martial law in Poland.

December 20th: Sixteen die after the Penlee lifeboat sinks off Cornwall's coast.

SPORT IN 1981

English Division One football champions: Aston Villa; runners-up: Ipswich Town

English FA Cup final: Tottenham Hotspur 3 Manchester City 2 (in a replay)

English League Cup Final: Liverpool 2 West Ham United 1 (in a replay)

Scottish Premier League football champions: Glasgow Celtic; runners-up: Aberdeen

Scottish FA Cup final: Glasgow Rangers 4 Dundee United 1 (in a replay)

Scottish League Cup final: Dundee United 3 Dundee 0

Irish League football champions: Glentoran; Irish Cup final: Ballymena United 1 Glenavon 0

League Of Ireland football champions: Athlone Town; cup winners: Dundalk

European Cup final: Liverpool 1 Real Madrid 0

European Cup-Winners' Cup final: Dinamo Tbilisi 2 Carl Zeiss Jena 1

UEFA Cup final: Ipswich Town beat AZ Alkmaar 5–4 on aggregate

English county cricket champions: Nottinghamshire

Five Nations' rugby union champions: France (the 'grand slam')

Formula One world drivers' champion: Nelson Piquet (Brazil) in a Brabham car

Gaelic football All-Ireland champions: Kerry; runners-up: Offaly

British Open golf champion: Bill Rogers (at Royal St. George's)

US Masters golf champion: Tom Watson

US Open golf champion: David Graham

USPGA golf champion: Larry Nelson

Rugby league Challenge Cup final: Widnes 18 Hull Kingston Rovers 9

Wimbledon men's singles tennis final: J McEnroe beat B Borg 4–6, 7–6, 7–6, 6–4

Wimbledon ladies' singles tennis final: C Evert beat H Mandlikova 6–2, 6–2

World snooker final: Steve Davis (England) beat Doug Mountjoy (Wales) 18–12

The Aintree Grand National steeplechase winner: Aldaniti; price 10–1

The Epsom Derby winner: Shergar; jockey – Walter Swinburn; price 10–11F

The Ryder Cup: Europe 9.5 The United States Of America 18.5

1981's BUCKET-KICKERS

January 6th: Archibald Joseph Cronin (British author); aged 84

January 23rd: Samuel Barber (US composer); aged 70

February 9th: Bill Haley (US singer); aged 55

March 9th: Sir Maurice Oldfield (British intelligence); aged 65

March 23rd: Field Marshal Sir Claude John Eyre Auchinleck (British soldier); aged 96

March 23rd: Mike Hailwood (British biker); aged 40

March 30th: De Witt Wallace (US publisher); aged 91

April 8th: General Omar Nelson Bradley (US soldier); aged 88

April 12th: Joe Louis Barrow (US boxer); aged 66

May 5th: Robert Gerard Sands (Irish terrorist); aged 27

May 11th: Robert Nesta Marley (Jamaican singer); aged 36

May 28th: Cardinal Stefan Wyszynski (Polish primate); aged 79

May 30th: Ziaur Rahman (Bangladesh's President); aged 45

August 1st: Omar Efrain Torrijos Herrera (Panama's dictator); aged 52

August 14th: Karl Bohm (Austrian conductor); aged 86

August 19th: Jessie Matthews (British actress); aged 74

September 1st: Albert Speer (German architect); aged 76

September 7th: Christy Brown (Irish author); aged 49

October 6th: Mohammed Anwar el-Sadat (Egypt's President); aged 62

November 10th: Abel Gance (French director); aged 92

November 14th: Reverend Robert Bradford (British politician); aged 40

November 16th: William Holden (US actor); aged 63

November 29th: Natalie Wood (US actress); aged 43

December 27th: Hoagy Carmichael (US pianist); aged 82

The song of the month for January 1982

Golden Brown by The Stranglers (peak chart position: No.2)

Apparently this song is about drugs, which comes as no surprise, since lead vocalist Hugh Cornwell had 'form' where illegal substances were concerned. Regardless of whether or not this item dealt with heroin, many British record buyers were addicted to this single with its waltz sound. The Stranglers had clearly come a long way since 'Peaches' and their punk origins. A two week stay at Number 2 was the very least this tune merited.

The song of the month for February 1982

See You by Depeche Mode (peak chart position: No.6)

Keyboardist Vince Clarke may have musically eloped with Alison Moyet for their Yazoo venture, but Depeche Mode kept the hits coming at regular intervals. 'See You' was a slightly different love song than the norm but it deservedly took Basildon's biggest export back to the British Top Ten. The Mode continued to carve out their own pop niche with the masterful 'Master And Servant' and the sensitive 'Shake The Disease' in ensuing years.

The song of the month for March 1982

My Camera Never Lies by Bucks Fizz (peak chart position: No.1)

Bucks Fizz had emulated the likes of Sandie Shaw and the Brotherhood Of Man by providing the United Kingdom with a success at the Eurovision Song Contest. One year later and Britain's latest unconvincing answer to Abba had notched up three British chart-toppers. The best of this trio was arguably 'My Camera Never Lies'. It is a half-decent pop song which certainly found favour with record purchasers who helped it to Number 1 for a week.

The song of the month for April 1982

I Love Rock 'N' Roll by Joan Jett And The Blackhearts
(peak chart position: No.4)

In Jamaican rastafarian culture, blackhearts are dreads who are to be feared. Joan Jett's own particular Blackhearts managed to offer a slice of rock which had a cross-over appeal both in rock and pop circles. This was one of those sing-along anthems that belonged in a pub jukebox. Americans were particularly impressed as Joan Jett and her gang were rewarded with a seven-week stint at the summit of the Billboard chart.

The song of the month for May 1982

I've Never Been To Me by Charlene (peak chart position: No.1)

This one-hit wonder was actually a product of the Motown hits factory, though it sounded nothing like Motown's typical dance tunes or soul records. Instead of which Charlene laments of her livelihood as a high-class hooker which prevented her from settling down and having a normal existence with a loving husband and doting children. Far from being sugary, this is a fantastic ballad with equally good music. More hits should have followed.

The song of the month for June 1982

Avalon by Roxy Music (peak chart position: No.13)

Bryan Ferry appeared to have a twin track approach to the music business. On the one hand, he carved out a solo career based largely on cover versions. On the other hand, the ex-art teacher displayed his creative side in association with Roxy Music. The band's latest project was entitled 'Avalon'. The album featured the excellent 'More Than This' but my preference is for the title track which must rate as one of the ultimate ambient pop recordings.

The song of the month for July 1982

It Started With A Kiss by Hot Chocolate (peak chart position: No.5)

Hot Chocolate had been regular visitors to the British hit parade for the last decade, proving that they were everybody's cup of tea. Back in 1980, Errol and the team narrowly missed out on a Number One with 'No Doubt About It' but they were back in a lofty UK chart position again with the sweet 'It Started With A Kiss'. It was a testimony to the band's longevity that they varied their material from the raunchy to more sensitive items.

The song of the month for August 1982

Save A Prayer by Duran Duran (peak chart position: No.2)

'Save A Prayer' is a definite front-runner for the award of 'the best song of 1982', but perhaps this wouldn't be difficult as pop world was inhabited by the likes of Renee And Renato, Musical Youth, the Goombay Dance Band, and Tight Fit. Nevertheless, this five and a half minute epic is the definitive New Romantics' single. The exotic video was filmed in Asia which the eye-catching Brummies passed through en route to world domination.

The song of the month for September 1982

Gypsy by Fleetwood Mac (peak chart position: No.46)

The self-styled gypsy Stevie Nicks succeeded in mesmerising Fleetwood Mac followers with the marvel called 'Gypsy' which was a highlight of the supergroup's new long player, Mirage, which had the unenviable task of living up to the commercial and critical heights of the quintet's three previous studio albums. For some bizarre reason, Britain was slow to buy several classic Fleetwood Mac hits until 'Tango Of The Night' appeared in 1987.

The song of the month for October 1982

Ruby Baby by Donald Fagen (not released as a single)

Donald Fagen had previously decorated the sound of Steely Dan with his vocals and keyboard sounds before he pursued the new frontier of a solo record. The result was the forty-minute delight, entitled 'The Nightfly', which is one of the greatest albums of the 1980s. This long player consisted largely of feel-good music with a jazz-pop fusion. Amongst the eight jewels is the gem, 'Ruby Baby'. This re-working of an old Leiber and Stoller tune is not only an infectious dance song, but it ought to be a candidate for the best cover version of all time.

The song of the month for November 1982

Poor Tom by Led Zeppelin (not released as a single)

This recording had been completed a dozen years earlier, but it was criminally over-looked by rock's fearsome foursome until the band's lead guitarist and producer Jimmy Page included it in the 'posthumous' compilation, 'Coda', which was released in November 1982. The 8 tracks varied in quality, with 'Poor Tom' being the pick of the LP. Here Page goes all acoustic, Robert Plant blows up a storm on mouth organ and John Bonham's drums are superb.

The song of the month for December 1982

Beat Surrender by The Jam (peak chart position: No.1)

Paul, Rick and Bruce decided to quit while they were ahead by going their separate ways whilst their band were still supremely successful and popular. Woking's greatest trio clocked out with 'Beat Surrender' which was not a mournful goodbye but an up-tempo farewell which lit up the charts in December 1982, only to be eclipsed by the dreadful 'Save Your Love'. Ah yes, British record-buyers were expressing their sense of humour again.

THE TOP 10 BEST SELLING UK SINGLES OF 1982

1 Come On Eileen by Dexy's Midnight Runners
2 Fame by Irene Cara
3 Eye Of The Tiger by Survivor
4 Do You Really Want To Hurt Me by Culture Club
5 The Lion Sleeps Tonight by Tight Fit
6 Pass The Dutchie by Musical Youth
7 I Don't Wanna Dance by Eddy Grant
8 Seven Tears by Goombay Dance Band
9 Ebony And Ivory by Paul McCartney & Stevie Wonder
10 Town Called Malice/Precious by The Jam

ALBUM OF THE YEAR FOR 1982

New Gold Dream (81–82–83–84) by Simple Minds
(released in September)

Side 1:

1. Someone, Somewhere in Summertime; 4:36
2. Colours Fly and Catherine Wheel; 3:49
3. Promised You A Miracle; 4:28
4. Big Sleep; 5:00
5. Somebody Up There Likes You; 5:02

Side 2:

1. New Gold Dream (81–82–83–84); 5:39
2. Glittering Prize; 4:33
3. Hunter and the Hunted; 5:55
4. King Is White and in the Crowd; 7:00

This majestic recording occupies its very own niche. It is almost inconceivable that a bunch of working-class Glaswegian blokes could compose such ambient items, but Simple Minds proved to be anything but simple. Whilst Jim Kerr's vocals are frequently blurred, the music is of the highest quality. 'Somebody Up There Likes You' is a delicious instrumental, whilst the title track is equally impressive. The guitar outro on 'Hunter and the Hunted' is also a joy to behold. Kerr is actually to be heard at the end of the marvellous 'Promised You A Miracle' suggesting that "Anything is possible". I believe him. This is one of those records which is indescribably outstanding. In fact, the word enchanting does spring to mind. Before U2 delivered 'The Joshua Tree' with its sombre moods, Simple Minds had got there first – five years earlier.

THE UK NUMBER ONE ALBUMS
OF 1982

09 Jan: Human League – Dare!;	3 weeks
30 Jan: Barbra Streisand – Love Songs;	7 weeks
20 Mar: The Jam – The Gift;	1 week
27 Mar: Barbra Streisand – Love Songs;	2 weeks
10 Apr: Iron Maiden – The Number Of The Beast;	2 weeks
24 Apr: Status Quo – 1982;	1 week
01 May: Barry Manilow – Barry Live In Britain;	1 week
08 May: Paul McCartney – Tug Of War;	2 weeks
22 May: Madness – Complete Madness;	2 weeks
05 Jun: Roxy Music – Avalon;	1 week
12 Jun: Madness – Complete Madness;	1 week
19 Jun: Roxy Music – Avalon;	2 weeks
03 Jul: ABC – The Lexicon Of Love;	3 weeks
24 Jul: Original Soundtrack – Fame;	2 weeks
07 Aug: Kids From Fame – The Kids From Fame;	8 weeks
02 Oct: Dire Straits – Love Over Gold;	4 weeks
30 Oct: Kids From Fame – The Kids From Fame;	4 weeks
27 Nov: Abba – The Singles – The First Ten Years;	1 week
04 Dec: John Lennon – The John Lennon Collection;	6 weeks

THE US NUMBER ONE ALBUMS OF 1982

02 Jan: AC/DC – For Those About To Rock We Salute You;	2 weeks
16 Jan: Foreigner – 4;	3 weeks
06 Feb: J. Geils Band – Freeze Frame;	4 weeks
06 Mar: The Go-Go's – Beauty And The Beat;	6 weeks
17 Apr: Vangelis / Soundtrack – Chariots Of Fire;	4 weeks
15 May: Asia – Asia;	2 weeks
29 May: Paul McCartney – Tug Of War;	3 weeks
19 Jun: Asia – Asia;	7 weeks
07 Aug: Fleetwood Mac – Mirage;	5 weeks
11 Sep: John Cougar – American Fool;	9 weeks
13 Nov: Men At Work – Business As Usual;	7 weeks

THE UK NUMBER ONE SINGLES
OF 1982

16 Jan: Bucks Fizz – Land Of Make Believe;	2 weeks
30 Jan: Shakin' Stevens – Oh Julie;	1 week
06 Feb: Kraftwerk – The Model/Computer Love;	1 week
13 Feb: The Jam – Town Called Malice/Precious;	3 weeks
06 Mar: Tight Fit – The Lion Sleeps Tonight;	3 weeks
27 Mar: Goombay Dance Band – Seven Tears;	3 weeks
17 Apr: Bucks Fizz – My Camera Never Lies;	1 week
24 Apr: Paul McCartney & Stevie Wonder – Ebony And Ivory;	3 weeks
15 May: Nicole – A Little Peace;	2 weeks
29 May: Madness – House Of Fun;	2 weeks
12 Jun: Adam Ant – Goody Two Shoes;	2 weeks
26 Jun: Charlene – I've Never Been To Me;	1 week
03 Jul: Captain Sensible – Happy Talk;	2 weeks
17 Jul: Irene Cara – Fame;	3 weeks
07 Aug: Dexy's Midnight Runners – Come On Eileen;	4 weeks
04 Sep: Survivor – Eye Of The Tiger;	4 weeks
02 Oct: Musical Youth – Pass The Dutchie;	3 weeks
23 Oct: Culture Club – Do You Really Want To Hurt Me;	3 weeks
13 Nov: Eddy Grant – I Don't Wanna Dance;	3 weeks
04 Dec: The Jam – Beat Surrender;	2 weeks
18 Dec: Renee & Renato – Save Your Love;	4 weeks

THE US NUMBER ONE SINGLES OF 1982

02 Jan: Olivia Newton-John – Physical;	4 weeks
30 Jan: Daryl Hall & John Oates – I Can't Go For That (No Can Do);	1 week
06 Feb: J. Geils Band – Centerfold;	6 weeks
20 Mar: Joan Jett & The Blackhearts – I Love Rock 'N Roll;	7 weeks
08 May: Vangelis – Chariots Of Fire;	1 week
15 May: Paul McCartney & Stevie Wonder – Ebony And Ivory;	7 weeks
03 Jul: Human League – Don't You Want Me;	3 weeks
24 Jul: Survivor – Eye Of The Tiger;	6 weeks
04 Sep: Steve Miller Band – Abracadabra;	1 week
11 Sep: Chicago – Hard To Say I'm Sorry;	2 weeks
25 Sep: Steve Miller Band – Abracadabra;	1 week
02 Oct: John Cougar – Jack And Diane;	4 weeks
30 Oct: Men At Work – Who Can It Be Now?;	1 week
06 Nov: Joe Cocker & Jennifer Warnes – Up Where We Belong;	3 weeks
27 Nov: Lionel Richie – Truly;	2 weeks
11 Dec: Toni Basil – Mickey;	1 week
18 Dec: Daryl Hall And John Oates – Maneater;	2 weeks

THE 'UNSUCCESSFUL' UK NUMBER TWO SINGLES OF 1982

13 Feb: The Stranglers – Golden Brown;	2 weeks
06 Mar: Toni Basil – Mickey;	2 weeks
03 Apr: Imagination – Just An Illusion;	1 week
17 Apr: Chas And Dave – Ain't No Pleasing You;	1 week
01 May: Bardo – One Step Further;	1 week
08 May: England World Cup Squad – This Time (We'll Get It Right);	1 week
22 May: Yazoo – Only You;	1 week
19 Jun: Soft Cell – Torch;	1 week
10 Jul: Steve Miller Band – Abracadabra;	2 weeks
24 Jul: Trio – Da Da Da;	1 week
11 Sep: Duran Duran – Save A Prayer;	1 week
18 Sep: Dire Straits – Private Investigations;	1 week
25 Sep: The Jam – The Bitterest Pill (I Ever Had To Swallow);	2 weeks
09 Oct: Fat Larry's Band – Zoom;	1 week
30 Oct: Kid Creole & The Coconuts – Annie I'm Not Your Daddy;	1 week
13 Nov: Dionne Warwick – Heartbreaker;	2 weeks
27 Nov: Human League – Mirror Man;	3 weeks
25 Dec: Shakin' Stevens – The Shakin' Stevens E.P.;	2 weeks

THE 'UNSUCCESSFUL' US NUMBER TWO SINGLES OF 1982

27 Feb: Journey – Open Arms

10 Apr: The Go-Gos – We Got The Beat

22 May: Rick Springfield – Don't Talk To Strangers

03 Jul: Toto – Rosanna

07 Aug: John Cougar – Hurts So Good

27 Nov: Laura Branigan – Gloria

NEWS HIGHLIGHTS OF 1982

January 12th: Mark Thatcher goes missing in the Sahara Desert.

January 21st: Britain's coal miners vote against strike action.

January 26th: Unemployment in Britain now exceeds three million.

February 17th: Robert Mugabe dismisses Joshua Nkomo from his cabinet.

February 19th: John De Lorean's Belfast car firm goes into receivership.

February 20th: Charles Haughey regains the Irish premiership.

March 4th: The Queen opens London's Barbican Centre arts complex.

March 25th: Roy Jenkins wins the Glasgow Hillhead by-election.

March 25th: Nicaragua's Sandinista government declares a state of emergency.

April 2nd: Argentine troops invade the Falkland Islands, seizing Port Stanley.

April 5th: Britain's task force sets sail while the Foreign Secretary resigns.

April 15th: The five murderers of President Sadat are executed in Cairo.

May 2nd: Hundreds are killed when the British sink the General Belgrano.

May 29th: The Pope pays a visit to Canterbury Cathedral.

May 30th: Spain joins the North Atlantic Treaty Organisation.

June 9th: The British twenty pence coin goes into circulation.

June 14th: The Falklands dispute ends in an Argentinian surrender.

June 21st: Princess Diana gives birth to a baby boy.

July 7th: Michael Fagan intrudes his way into the Queen's bedroom.

July 7th: David Moorcroft breaks the 5,000 metres world record.

July 20th: IRA bombs explode in Hyde Park and Regent's Park.

August 21st: The PLO begins to evacuate Beirut.

August 23rd: Bashir Gemayel is elected President of Lebanon.

August 30th: Yassir Arafat flees Beirut, under pressure from the Israeli forces.

September 14th: Bashir Gemayel is assassinated by a bomb.

September 18th: Civilians are massacred in two Palestinian Beirut camps.

September 22nd: Margaret Thatcher pays a visit to Peking.

October 1st: Helmut Kohl replaces Helmut Schmidt as West German Chancellor.

October 11th: The Mary Rose is raised from its watery grave.

October 28th: Felipe Gonzalez and his Socialists win Spain's general election.

November 2nd: Channel Four begins broadcasting with the 'Countdown' show.

November 11th: Nationalists boycott the opening of Northern Ireland's Assembly.

November 12th: Lech Walesa is released from detention.

December 12th: About 20,000 women encircle the Greenham Common airbase.

December 15th: Gibraltar's border with Spain is re-opened.

December 30th: England beat Australia by a paltry three runs at Melbourne.

SPORT IN 1982

English Division One football champions: Liverpool; runners-up: Ipswich Town

English FA Cup final: Tottenham Hotspur 1 Queen's Park Rangers 0 (in a replay)

English League Cup Final: Liverpool 3 Tottenham Hotspur 1 (after extra time)

Scottish Premier League football champions: Glasgow Celtic; runners-up: Aberdeen

Scottish FA Cup final: Aberdeen 4 Glasgow Rangers 1 (after extra time)

Scottish League Cup final: Glasgow Rangers 2 Dundee United 1

Irish League football champions: Linfield; Irish Cup final: Linfield 2 Coleraine 1

League Of Ireland football champions: Dundalk; cup winners: Limerick United

European Cup final: Aston Villa 1 Bayern Munich 0

European Cup-Winners' Cup final: Barcelona 2 Standard de Liege 1

UEFA Cup final: IFK Goteborg beat Hamburg 4–0 on aggregate

English county cricket champions: Middlesex

Five Nations' rugby union champions: Ireland (the 'triple crown')

Formula One world drivers' champion: Keke Rosberg (Finland) in a Williams car

Gaelic football All-Ireland champions: Offaly; runners-up: Kerry

British Open golf champion: Tom Watson (at Royal Troon)

US Masters golf champion: Craig Stadler

US Open golf champion: Tom Watson

USPGA golf champion: Raymond Floyd

Rugby league Challenge Cup final: Hull 18 Widnes 9 (in a replay)

Wimbledon men's singles tennis final: J Connors beat J McEnroe 3–6, 6–3, 6–7, 7–6, 6–4

Wimbledon ladies' singles tennis final: M Navratilova beat C Evert 6–1, 3–6, 6–2

World snooker final: Alex Higgins (Northern Ireland) beat Ray Reardon (Wales) 18–15

The Aintree Grand National steeplechase winner: Grittar; price 7–1F

The Epsom Derby winner: Golden Fleece; jockey – Pat Eddery; price 3–1F

Football World Cup final: Italy 3 West Germany 1 (in Madrid)

1982's BUCKET-KICKERS

February 17th: Thelonius Monk (US pianist); aged 64

March 8th: Richard Austin 'Rab' Butler (British politician); aged 79

March 29th: Carl Orff (German composer); aged 86

May 29th: Romy Schneider (Austrian actress); aged 43

June 10th: Rainer Werner Fassbinder (German director); aged 36

June 16th: James Honeyman-Scott (British musician); aged 25

August 12th: Henry Fonda (US actor); aged 77

August 21st: King Sobhuza II of Swaziland; aged 83

August 29th: Ingrid Bergman (Swedish actress); aged 67

September 1st: Wladyslaw Gomulka (ex-Polish Premier); aged 77

September 5th: Group Captain Sir Douglas Robert Steuart Bader
(British airman); aged 72

September 14th: Princess Grace of Monaco (US actress); aged 52

October 4th: Glenn Gould (Canadian pianist); aged 50

November 5th: Jacques Tati (French director); aged 74

November 10th: Leonid Brezhnev (Soviet statesman); aged 75

November 16th: Arthur Bowden Askey (British comedian); aged 82

December 20th: Artur Rubinstein (US pianist); aged 95

The song of the month for January 1983

Billie Jean by Michael Jackson (peak chart position: No.1)

'Wacko Jacko' scored his second British chart-topper when 'Billie Jean' paved the way for the enduring appeal of the epic 'Thriller' album. The song kick starts with that unforgettable drum beat that ushers in a dancefloor treasure that became a staple of many an eighties discotheque. Jackson was consolidating his reputation as the best male vocalist on the planet. His solo career was going into orbit, while his personality did likewise.

The song of the month for February 1983

Total Eclipse Of The Heart by Bonnie Tyler (peak chart position: No.1)

Bonnie Tyler was the latest singing sensation from the principality of Wales, following the hallowed footsteps of Shirley Bassey and Tom Jones. Bonnie had enjoyed a number of flirtations with the hit parade in the late 1970s but her finest five minutes came courtesy of the outstanding 'Total Eclipse Of The Heart'. This track was a reminder to detractors of the merits of eighties music, as it totally eclipsed all the other singles in the UK chart.

The song of the month for March 1983

Blue Monday by New Order (peak chart position: No.9)

The three surviving members of the far from joyful Joy Division eventually recovered from the shattering loss of Ian Curtis and subsequently instigated a new order of indie dance music, with the assistance of new recruit, Gillian Gilbert. Their first major triumph was 'Blue Monday' which spent dozens of weeks on the hit parade, thus rendering it the most successful single to be released by an independent label, namely Factory Records.

The song of the month for April 1983
Church Of The Poison Mind by Culture Club (peak chart position: No 2)

Culture Club's latest toe-tapper invited comparisons with the trademark Motown sound. This description did not by any means flatter this fine tune. It may not have reached the pop summit but it was at least as good as the huge-selling 'Karma Chameleon' that did arrive there several months later. The lyrics are fairly forgettable but the rhythm and the harmonica input from Jud Lander were a real joy for my own poison mind.

The song of the month for May 1983
Buffalo Soldier by Bob Marley And The Wailers (peak chart position: No.4)

Robert Nesta Marley had been firmly ensconced in his mausoleum at St.Ann's in rural Jamaica for the last two years, but the reggae superstar was still able to make his charismatic presence felt beyond the grave. 'Buffalo Soldier' was the key track from the posthumous compilation of unreleased material that comprised the 'Confrontation' album. Marley was able to successfully confront all chart competitors with this 'new' song which told the story of how black Americans were recruited to fight for the Union in the American Civil War.

The song of the month for June 1983
China Girl by David Bowie (peak chart position: No.2)

The ever-changing Bowie was now operating under the new alias of David Bowie. Casting off all his previous costumes and personas, the great Bowie showed that when it came to dance music, he could still cut it. Following on from the success of 'Let's Dance', Bowie covered his old mate Iggy Pop's 'China Girl' which had previously been performed in 1977. Not content with a majestic pop song, Bowie proceeded to trouble the censor with his nude re-enactment of 'From Here To Eternity' at the conclusion of the song's excellent video.

The song of the month for July 1983

Double Dutch by Malcolm McLaren (peak chart position: No.3)

Hardly one of the world's great vocalists, Malcolm McLaren nevertheless enjoyed chart success with 'Buffalo Gals' and the wonderful 'Double Dutch' which was a celebration of a new American dance craze. McLaren had previously sang 'You Need Hands', an old Max Bygraves number on 'The Great Rock 'N' Roll Swindle' soundtrack. After the success of 'Double Dutch', McLaren was embroiled in a losing battle with his old adversary Johnny Rotten in a protracted legal dispute arising out of the break-up of the notorious Sex Pistols.

The song of the month for August 1983

Gold by Spandau Ballet (peak chart position: No.2)

Spandau Ballet were one of the standard bearers of the New Romantics' pop craze. They peaked in the middle of 1983 with the impressive chart-topper, 'True'. Drawn from the same album was 'Gold' which was a worthy follow-up. Although 'Gold' had to settle for the silver medal position on the singles chart podium, it still stands the test of time as one of the great pop songs of the much-maligned 'eighties.

The song of the month for September 1983

Come Back And Stay by Paul Young (peak chart position: No.4)

Paul Young had previously served his musical apprenticeship alongside the Q-Tips, before he plotted what would be a successful solo path. Young's big breakthrough came with 'Wherever I Lay My Hat (That's My Home)' but I have a stronger liking for his next smash hit, 'Come Back And Stay' which benefited from backing vocals from female duo, Kim and Maz. This hit was written by Jack Lee, author of Blondie's 'Hanging On The Telephone'.

The song of the month for October 1983
Uptown Girl by Billy Joel (peak chart position: No 1)

Billy Joel came along with an unlikely dancefloor favourite which succeeded in terminating Karma Chameleon's six week occupation of the British Number One position. In the process, Joel found he had created the second biggest-selling UK single of 1983. Not just a great reason for swaying your feet and hips to, 'Uptown Girl' featured Joel's model girlfriend Christie Brinkley in a video that included a brilliant choreography routine.

The song of the month for November 1983
Thank You For The Music by Abba (peak chart position: No.33)

The turbulent singing career of Abba drew to a close with the appropriate 'Thank You For The Music'. The fab four may have enjoyed phenomenal success, but they paid for it with the price of relationship turmoil. Thus when the greatest singles act of the 1970s took their bow, they were heartily sick of one another, and judging by the song's uncharacteristic failure in the hit parade, their once devoted public were tired of them too. Ironically, this is one of their best compositions sung by Agnetha, the "bit of a bore" "with the golden hair".

The song of the month for December 1983
Many Rivers To Cross by UB40 (peak chart position: No.16)

Not content with treating British music lovers to the year's third biggest-selling single, 'Red Red Wine', UB40 returned in mid-winter with a less successful incursion into the Yuletide charts. 'Many Rivers To Cross' had previously been performed by Jamaican reggae legend Jimmy Cliff on the movie, 'The Harder They Come'. UB40 recorded a magnificent soulful version which deserved a much bigger splash in the hit parade than it achieved.

THE TOP 10 BEST SELLING UK SINGLES OF 1983

1 Karma Chameleon by Culture Club

2 Uptown Girl by Billy Joel

3 Red Red Wine by UB40

4 Let's Dance by David Bowie

5 Total Eclipse Of The Heart by Bonnie Tyler

6 Down Under by Men At Work

7 Billie Jean by Michael Jackson

8 True by Spandau Ballet

9 All Night Long (All Night) by Lionel Richie

10 You Can't Hurry Love by Phil Collins

ALBUM OF THE YEAR FOR 1983

Labour Of Love by UB40 (released in September)

Side 1:	Side 2:
1. Cherry Oh Baby; 3:18	1. Red Red Wine; 5:21
2. Keep on Moving; 4:37	2. Guilty; 3:16
3. Please Don't Make Me Cry; 3:26	3. She Caught the Train; 3:17
4. Sweet Sensation; 3:42	4. Version Girl; 3:27
5. Johnny Too Bad; 4:57	5. Many Rivers To Cross; 4:31

Birmingham's finest octet had begun to flounder after the initial successes of 'Signing Off' and the trio of hit singles which richly contributed to the airwaves in 1980. By 1983 the group went back to their roots and recorded an album entirely of covers in tribute to the Jamaican artists who had provided them with joy and pleasure in their youth. The mysterious Dr.X explains this perfectly eloquently on the album sleeve. Forsaking their political stance, the lads concentrate on the well-worn formula of songs about falling in and out of love. The magnificent 'Guilty', the Top Ten hit single 'Please Don't Make Me Cry', and 'She Caught The Train' all visit the familiar pop territory of unrequited love, but their own reggae input is most refreshing. Above all, the combo actually benefit from prominent keyboards on the likes of 'Johnny Too Bad' and 'Keep On Moving'. Regrettably the band subsequently allowed their sound to be suffocated by an over-reliance on brass instruments. Meanwhile, 'Red Red Wine' is not only a peach of a recording, but the accompanying black and white video merits repeated viewing, even if the rest of the 'Labour Of Love' film is mediocre.

THE UK NUMBER ONE ALBUMS
OF 1983

15 Jan: Various artist comp. (Ronco) – Raiders Of The Pop Charts;	2 weeks
29 Jan: Men At Work – Business As Usual;	5 weeks
05 Mar: Michael Jackson – Thriller;	1 week
12 Mar: U2 – War;	1 week
19 Mar: Michael Jackson – Thriller;	1 week
26 Mar: Tears For Fears – The Hurting;	1 week
02 Apr: Pink Floyd – The Final Cut;	2 weeks
16 Apr: Bonnie Tyler – Faster Than The Speed Of Night;	1 week
23 Apr: David Bowie – Let's Dance;	3 weeks
14 May: Spandau Ballet – True;	1 week
21 May: Michael Jackson – Thriller;	5 weeks
25 Jun: The Police – Synchronicity;	2 weeks
09 Jul: Wham! – Fantastic!;	2 weeks
23 Jul: Yazoo – You And Me Both;	2 weeks
06 Aug: The Beach Boys – The Very Best Of The Beach Boys;	2 weeks
20 Aug: Michael Jackson Plus The Jackson Five – 18 Greatest Hits;	3 weeks
10 Sep: The Beach Boys – The Very Best Of The Beach Boys;	1 week
17 Sep: Paul Young – No Parlez;	1 week
24 Sep: UB40 – Labour Of Love;	1 week
01 Oct: Paul Young – No Parlez;	2 weeks
15 Oct: Genesis – Genesis;	1 week
22 Oct: Culture Club – Colour By Numbers;	3 weeks
12 Nov: Lionel Richie – Can't Slow Down;	1 week
19 Nov: Culture Club – Colour By Numbers;	2 weeks
03 Dec: Duran Duran – Seven And The Ragged Tiger;	1 week
10 Dec: Paul Young – No Parlez;	1 week
17 Dec: Various artist comp. (EMI/Virgin) – Now That's What I Call Music;	3 weeks

THE US NUMBER ONE ALBUMS OF 1983

01 Jan: Men At Work – Business As Usual;	8 weeks
26 Feb: Michael Jackson – Thriller;	17 weeks
25 Jun: Soundtrack – Flashdance;	2 weeks
09 Jul: Michael Jackson – Thriller;	2 weeks
23 Jul: The Police – Synchronicity;	7 weeks
10 Sep: Michael Jackson – Thriller;	1 week
17 Sep: The Police – Synchronicity;	10 weeks
26 Nov: Quiet Riot – Metal Health;	1 week
03 Dec: Lionel Richie – Can't Slow Down;	3 weeks
24 Dec: Michael Jackson – Thriller;	2 weeks

THE UK NUMBER ONE SINGLES
OF 1983

15 Jan: Phil Collins – You Can't Hurry Love;	2 weeks
29 Jan: Men At Work – Down Under;	3 weeks
19 Feb: Kajagoogoo – Too Shy;	2 weeks
05 Mar: Michael Jackson – Billie Jean;	1 week
12 Mar: Bonnie Tyler – Total Eclipse Of The Heart;	2 weeks
26 Mar: Duran Duran – Is There Something I Should Know;	2 weeks
09 Apr: David Bowie – Let's Dance;	3 weeks
30 Apr: Spandau Ballet – True;	4 weeks
28 May: New Edition – Candy Girl;	1 week
04 Jun: The Police – Every Breath You Take;	4 weeks
02 Jul: Rod Stewart – Baby Jane;	3 weeks
23 Jul: Paul Young – Wherever I Lay My Hat;	3 weeks
13 Aug: K C And The Sunshine Band – Give It Up;	3 weeks
03 Sep: UB40 – Red Red Wine;	3 weeks
24 Sep: Culture Club – Karma Chameleon;	6 weeks
05 Nov: Billy Joel – Uptown Girl;	5 weeks
10 Dec: Flying Pickets – Only You;	5 weeks

THE US NUMBER ONE SINGLES OF 1983

01 Jan: Daryl Hall & John Oates – Maneater;	2 weeks
15 Jan: Men At Work – Down Under;	3 weeks
05 Feb: Toto – Africa;	1 week
12 Feb: Men At Work – Down Under;	1 week
19 Feb: Patti Austin & James Ingram – Baby, Come To Me;	2 weeks
05 Mar: Michael Jackson – Billie Jean;	7 weeks
23 Apr: Dexys Midnight Runners – Come On Eileen;	1 week
30 Apr: Michael Jackson – Beat It;	3 weeks
21 May: David Bowie – Let's Dance;	1 week
28 May: Irene Cara – Flashdance ... What A Feeling;	6 weeks
09 Jul: The Police – Every Breath You Take;	8 weeks
03 Sep: Eurythmics – Sweet Dreams (Are Made Of This);	1 week
10 Sep: Michael Sembello – Maniac;	2 weeks
24 Sep: Billy Joel – Tell Her About It;	1 week
01 Oct: Bonnie Tyler – Total Eclipse Of The Heart;	4 weeks
29 Oct: Kenny Rogers With Dolly Parton – Islands In The Stream;	2 weeks
12 Nov: Lionel Richie – All Night Long (All Night);	4 weeks
10 Dec: Paul McCartney & Michael Jackson – Say Say Say;	4 weeks

THE 'UNSUCCESSFUL' UK NUMBER TWO SINGLES OF 1983

15 Jan: David Essex – A Winter's Tale;	1 week
05 Feb: Eddy Grant – Electric Avenue;	1 week
19 Mar: Eurythmics – Sweet Dreams (Are Made Of This);	1 week
16 Apr: Culture Club – Church Of The Poison Mind;	2 weeks
30 Apr: FR David – Words;	2 weeks
14 May: Human League – (Keep Feeling) Fascination;	1 week
21 May: Heaven 17 – Temptation;	1 week
04 Jun: Wham! – Bad Boys;	2 weeks
18 Jun: David Bowie – China Girl;	1 week
09 Jul: Irene Cara – Flashdance (What A Feeling);	1 week
23 Jul: Freeez – I.O.U.;	3 weeks
20 Aug: Spandau Ballet – Gold;	2 weeks
10 Sep: Madness – Wings Of A Dove;	1 week
17 Sep: Peabo Bryson & Roberta Flack – Tonight I Celebrate My Love;	1 week
08 Oct: David Bowie – Modern Love;	1 week
15 Oct: Tracey Ullman – They Don't Know;	2 weeks
29 Oct: Lionel Richie – All Night Long (All Night);	3 weeks
19 Nov: Paul McCartney & Michael Jackson – Say Say Say;	2 weeks
03 Dec: Paul Young – Love Of The Common People;	3 weeks
24 Dec: Slade – My Oh My;	3 weeks

THE 'UNSUCCESSFUL' US NUMBER TWO SINGLES OF 1983

08 Jan: Michael Jackson & Paul McCartney – The Girl Is Mine

26 Feb: Bob Seger & The Silver Bullet Band – Shame On The Moon

26 Mar: Culture Club – Do You Really Want To Hurt Me

07 May: Greg Kihn – Jeopardy

18 Jun: Culture Club – Time (Clock Of The Heart)

02 Jul: Eddy Grant – Electric Avenue

06 Oct: Air Supply – Making Love Out Of Nothing At All

17 Dec: Daryl Hall & John Oates – Say It Isn't So

NEWS HIGHLIGHTS OF 1983

January 7th: Australia regain the cricket Ashes from England.
January 17th: 'Breakfast Time' begins broadcasting on BBC One.
January 26th: Bjorn Borg retires from competitive tennis, aged 26.
February 1st: ITV starts broadcasting its TV-am.
February 9th: The ex-Derby winner Shergar goes missing, feared kidnapped.
February 24th: Simon Hughes wins the Bermondsey and Southwark by-election.
March 1st: The Queen and Prince Philip visit President Reagan.
March 5th: Bob Hawke's Labour Party wins Australia's general election.
March 13th: Joshua Nkomo flees to London after intimidation from Mugabe.
April 1st: Thousands of protesters besiege Greenham Common.
April 19th: The American embassy in Beirut is destroyed by a bomb.
April 25th: The Socialist Party wins the Portuguese general election.
May 6th: The so-called 'Hitler Diaries' are exposed as a fake.
May 9th: Mrs Thatcher calls a general election for June the 9th.
May 16th: The first wheel clamps are introduced in central London.
June 10th: The Conservatives win by a landslide in Britain's general election.
June 11th: Nigel Lawson is appointed as the Chancellor of the Exchequer.
June 12th: Michael Foot resigns as the leader of Britain's Labour Party.
July 7th: Nigel Lawson announces huge spending cuts.
July 21st: Martial law is abolished in Poland.
July 25th: Rioting occurs in Sri Lanka between the Sinhalese and Tamils.
August 4th: Bettino Craxi becomes Italy's first Socialist Prime Minister.
August 10th: The first athletics world championships begin in Helsinki.
August 21st: Benigno Aquino, the rival of Ferdinand Marcos, is shot dead.
September 6th: The Soviets shoot down a Korean passenger airliner.
September 25th: Over 100 IRA prisoners escape from prison.
September 26th: Australia win yachting's Admirals' Cup for the first time.
October 2nd: Neil Kinnock is elected as the British Labour Party leader.
October 23rd: Two suicide bomb attacks kill almost 300 in Beirut.
October 26th: The invading American troops seize control of Grenada.
November 9th: Brewing magnate Alfred Heineken is kidnapped in Holland.
November 12th: Gerry Adams is elected as President of Sinn Fein.
November 30th: A police raid succeeds in freeing Alfred Heineken.
December 10th: Lech Walesa is awarded the Nobel Peace Prize in absentia.
December 10th: Military rule ends as Raul Alfonsin becomes Argentine President.
December 17th: An IRA bomb explodes outside Harrods in Knightsbridge.

SPORT IN 1983

English Division One football champions: Liverpool; runners-up: Watford

English FA Cup final: Manchester United 4 Brighton And Hove Albion 0 (in a replay)

English League Cup Final: Liverpool 2 Manchester United 1 (after extra time)

Scottish Premier League football champions: Dundee United; runners-up: Glasgow Celtic

Scottish FA Cup final: Aberdeen 1 Glasgow Rangers 0 (after extra time)

Scottish League Cup final: Glasgow Celtic 2 Glasgow Rangers 1

Irish League football champions: Linfield; Irish Cup final: Glentoran 2 Linfield 1 (in a replay)

League Of Ireland football champions: Athlone Town; cup winners: Sligo Rovers

European Cup final: Hamburg 1 Juventus 0

European Cup-Winners' Cup final: Aberdeen 2 Real Madrid 1 (after extra time)

UEFA Cup final: Anderlecht beat Benfica 2–1 on aggregate

English county cricket champions: Essex

Five Nations' rugby union champions: France and Ireland (both 6 points)

Formula One world drivers' champion: Nelson Piquet (Brazil) in a Brabham car

Gaelic football All-Ireland champions: Dublin; runners-up: Galway

British Open golf champion: Tom Watson (at Royal Birkdale)

US Masters golf champion: Seve Ballesteros

US Open golf champion: Larry Nelson

USPGA golf champion: Hal Sutton

Rugby league Challenge Cup final: Featherstone Rovers 14 Hull 12

Wimbledon men's singles tennis final: J McEnroe beat C Lewis 6–2, 6–2, 6–2

Wimbledon ladies' singles tennis final: M Navratilova beat A Jaeger 6–0, 6–3

World snooker final: Steve Davis (England) beat Cliff Thorburn (Canada) 18–6

The Aintree Grand National steeplechase winner: Corbiere; price 13–1

The Epsom Derby winner: Teenoso; jockey – Lester Piggott; price 9–2F

The Ryder Cup: The United States Of America 14.5 Europe 13.5

1983's BUCKET-KICKERS

January 11th: Nikolai Podgorny (Soviet statesman); aged 79

January 24th: George Cukor (US director); aged 83

February 25th: Tennessee Williams (US playwright); aged 71

March 3rd: Arthur Koestler (Hungarian author); aged 77

March 8th: Sir William Turner Walton (British composer); aged 80

March 15th: Dame Rebecca West (British author); aged 90

April 4th: Gloria Swanson (US actress); aged 84

April 14th: Pete Farndon (British musician); aged 30

May 21st: Lord Kenneth Clark (British historian); aged 79

May 31st: Jack Dempsey (US boxer); aged 87

July 29th: Luis Bunuel (Spanish director); aged 83

July 29th: James David Graham Niven (British actor); aged 73

August 21st: Benigno Aquino, Junior, (Filipino politician); aged 50

September 10th: Balthazar Johannes Vorster (ex-South African Prime Minister); aged 67

October 10th: Sir Ralph David Richardson (British actor); aged 80

October 19th: Maurice Rupert Bishop (Grenada's Prime Minister); aged 39

December 25th: Joan Miro (Spanish artist); aged 90

The song of the month for January 1984

What Difference Does It Make? by The Smiths (peak chart position: No.12)

A new pop phenomenon invaded the airwaves in 1983 when the Smiths reached out to the disillusioned youth with their own jangly guitar anthems which were frequently provocative, sometimes humorous, and never dull. The frontman Morrissey projected himself as the very antithesis of the teen pop idol, selling himself as a celibate and loveless individual. Against this background the Smiths issued the typically downbeat 'What Difference Does It Make?' In actual fact, Manchester's fab four did make a big difference over the next 4 years.

The song of the month for February 1984

Michael Caine by Madness (peak chart position: No.11)

Ever since 'The Prince' had wandered into the British Top Twenty in the autumn of 1979, Madness had been a constant presence in the UK hit parade with their fast-paced observations of the modern world, helped by eye-catching videos that revealed their own playfulness and sense of humour. By their own high standards, the admirable 'Michael Caine' was something of a commercial failure, even though the great man contributes a spoken part in the hit. Unfortunately for Madness, Mike Barson, their main songwriter, had departed the group and the remaining six soldiered on with decreasing success without him until they too decided to become sane.

The song of the month for March 1984

Nelson Mandela by The Special AKA (peak chart position: No.9)

Aside from being a fine dance track that deservedly sneaked into the British Top Ten, this historic anti-apartheid anthem was firm proof that music can change the world. Who in the youth market after all had ever heard of Nelson Mandela, incarcerated twenty years earlier? Not only did this commendable song bring renewed attention to the plight of Mandela, but the assembled cast of musicians including Elvis Costello and Dave Wakeling from The Beat were a prototype Band Aid several months before it too impacted upon the world.

The song of the month for April 1984

I Want To Break Free by Queen (peak chart position: No.3)

Scarcely a year elapsed without Queen making their considerable presence felt in pop world. 1984 was especially fruitful for Freddie and his gang as first 'Radio Ga Ga' climbed into the British Top Three and then not to be outdone, the memorable 'I Want To Break Free' did likewise. This belting tune profited from a superb instrumental break as well as a video in which the foursome camp it up in drag as a spoof of Coronation Street.

The song of the month for May 1984

Wake Me Up Before You Go Go by Wham! (peak chart position: No.1)

George Michael and the apparently less talented Andrew Ridgeley succeeded in becoming the new heart-throbs of planet pop and were consequently guaranteed a large volume of record sales from young females. As a result Wham! achieved a string of hits on both sides of the Atlantic as they acted as the perfect antidote to the artists who took themselves too seriously. The duo peaked with the popular 'Wake Me Up Before You Go Go.'

The song of the month for June 1984

Two Tribes by Frankie Goes To Hollywood (peak chart position: No.1)

If 1976 belonged to Abba, and 1981 was the year of Adam And The Ants, then 1984 was the twelve months when Frankie Goes To Hollywood could do no wrong. First they had the supreme good fortune of having their single 'Relax' banned by the BBC thus guaranteeing it Number One status and a lengthy residence in the charts and then Liverpool's latest sensations sat at the singles summit for a mere nine weeks with 'Two Tribes' which was their own tongue-in-cheek assessment of the Cold War. Such was their phenomenal success that the rest of us had to suffer the 'Frankie Says' tee-shirts for many months thereafter, so they had a lot to answer for.

The song of the month for July 1984

A Hole In My Shoe by Neil (peak chart position: No.2)

While the formidable 'Two Tribes' fought off all comers, some British record buyers found relief in yet another novelty record. 'A Hole In My Shoe' had originally appeared in the British singles chart in the late 'sixties for Traffic. This time around it was re-interpreted by Neil, alternatively known as Nigel Planer. Neil formed one quarter of the cult comedy outfit, 'The Young Ones' as the conscientious but morose hippie. What a pop idol!

The song of the month for August 1984

Careless Whisper by George Michael (peak chart position: No.1)

If Frankie's Holly Johnson and Paul Rutherford were dominating the UK singles chart in 1984, George Michael was staking his own valid claim to superstardom. George stepped away from his collaboration with Andrew and promptly delivered not only one of the great love songs of its era but also one of the best chart-toppers of the 1980s. It was clear from this offering that George could deliver mature, soulful ballads which would enable him to extend his musical career a long way beyond the limitations of Wham's no nonsense pop formula.

The song of the month for September 1984

Purple Rain by Prince (peak chart position: No.8)

This was a giant recording from a tiny man. The album version weighs in at more than eight and a half minutes and it is a fitting finale to an epic long player. Rarely has the electric guitar and the more conventional stringed instruments functioned better in unison than they did on 'Purple Rain'. The single did manage to find its way into the Top Ten of the charts on both sides of the Atlantic, and rightly so. Did the 'eighties produce a better track than this work of art?

The song of the month for October 1984

I'm Gonna Tear Your Playhouse Down by Paul Young
(peak chart position: No.9)

The hugely likeable Paul Young built upon the success of his 'No Parlez' long player with his next album, entitled 'The Secret Of Association'. Again this fine soul singer drew upon other material from the likes of Hall And Oates for the splendid 'Everytime You Go Away' and then he also had a bash at releasing the lively 'I'm Gonna Tear Your Playhouse Down'. Yet again, young Paul was aided by the backing vocals of Kim and Maz, 'the fabulous wealthy tarts'.

The song of the month for November 1984

All Through The Night by Cyndi Lauper (peak chart position: No.64)

British record-buyers spectacularly failed to pay due recognition to this wondrous single, which enjoyed better success on the other side of the 'big pond'. In my semi-humble opinion 'All Through The Night' ranks alongside 'Cruel Summer' by Bananarama and 'Take On Me' by A-ha for the imaginary prize of the best pop song of the decade. I remain perpetually puzzled why disc jockeys seem more smitten with the monotonous and infinitely inferior 'Time After Time'.

The song of the month for December 1984

Do They Know It's Christmas? by Band Aid (peak chart position: No.1)

Bob Geldof and Midge Ure had both visited the top of the British singles charts before, but this time they were so moved by the television news coverage of the deteriorating famine in Ethiopia that they launched a new musical venture in a ploy to raise funds for famine relief. Consequently they hastily summoned the top names in British pop to form the most famous choir in the history of music, modern and classical. 'Do They Know It's Christmas' is not only a well-intentioned recording, but its lyrics are thought-provoking. The song had such a colossal impact that it remained the biggest-selling tune in the history of the British charts until the death of Princess Diana almost 13 years later. This Band Aid smash hit was one glorious occasion when planet pop changed the world for the better.

THE TOP 10 BEST SELLING UK SINGLES OF 1984

1 Do They Know It's Christmas by Band Aid
2 I Just Called To Say I Love You by Stevie Wonder
3 Relax by Frankie Goes To Hollywood
4 Two Tribes by Frankie Goes To Hollywood
5 Careless Whisper by George Michael
6 Last Christmas by Wham!
7 Hello by Lionel Richie
8 Agadoo by Black Lace
9 Freedom by Wham!
10 Ghostbusters by Ray Parker Junior

ALBUM OF THE YEAR FOR 1984

Purple Rain by Prince And The Revolution (released in June)

Side 1:

1. Let's Go Crazy; 4:39
2. Take Me with U; 3:58
3. The Beautiful Ones; 5:17
4. Computer Blue; 3:56
5. Darling Nikki; 4:13

Side 2:

1. When Doves Cry; 5:52
2. I Would Die 4 U; 2:49
3. Baby I'm A Star; 4:24
4. Purple Rain; 8:41

"Ladies and gentlemen we are gathered here today, to get through this thing called" 'Purple Rain'. This long player is an obvious candidate for the accolade of the best album of the decade. Side One is flawless, right from the mock pulpit introduction of the pseudo-spiritual 'Let's Go Crazy' through to the risque 'Darling Nikki'. The temptress Nikki inspired a spoof version on 'The Fast Show' when a George Formby character performs his own 'interpretation'. It is surreal in the extreme. Meanwhile back in the real world, Prince and his Revolution pull off a successful coup with the fabulous 'When Doves Cry'. However, the fairest of them all is the title track which spectacularly brings the curtain down on the proceedings. It is not hard to comprehend why this LP is universally held in high regard. It is the glowing example of 'eighties pop music. 'Swinging 'sixties', eat your heart out!

THE UK NUMBER ONE ALBUMS
OF 1984

14 Jan: Paul Young – No Parlez;	1 week
21 Jan: Various artist comp. (EMI/Virgin) –	
Now That's What I Call Music;	1 week
28 Jan: Michael Jackson – Thriller;	1 week
04 Feb: Eurythmics – Touch;	2 weeks
18 Feb: Simple Minds – Sparkle In The Rain;	1 week
25 Feb: Thompson Twins – Into The Gap;	3 weeks
17 Mar: Howard Jones – Human's Lib;	2 weeks
31 Mar: Lionel Richie – Can't Slow Down;	2 weeks
14 Apr: Various artist comp. (Virgin/EMI) –	
Now That's What I Call Music II;	5 weeks
19 May: Bob Marley & The Wailers – Legend;	12 weeks
11 Aug: Various artist comp. (Virgin/EMI) –	
Now That's What I Call Music III;	8 weeks
06 Oct: David Bowie – Tonight;	1 week
13 Oct: U2 – The Unforgettable Fire;	2 weeks
27 Oct: Big Country – Steeltown;	1 week
03 Nov: Paul McCartney – Give My Regards To Broad Street (OST);	1 week
10 Nov: Frankie Goes To Hollywood – Welcome To The Pleasuredome;	1 week
17 Nov: Wham! – Make It Big;	2 weeks
01 Dec: Various artist comp. (CBS/WEA) –	
The Hits Album/The Hits Tape;	7 weeks

THE US NUMBER ONE ALBUMS OF 1984

07 Jan: Michael Jackson – Thriller;   15 weeks

21 Apr: Soundtrack – Footloose;   10 weeks

30 Jun: Huey Lewis & The News – Sports;   1 week

07 Jul: Bruce Springsteen – Born In The U.S.A.;   4 weeks

04 Aug: Prince And The Revolution – Purple Rain;   22 weeks

THE UK NUMBER ONE SINGLES
OF 1984

14 Jan: Paul McCartney – Pipes Of Peace;	2 weeks
28 Jan: Frankie Goes To Hollywood – Relax;	5 weeks
03 Mar: Nena – 99 Red Balloons;	3 weeks
24 Mar: Lionel Richie – Hello;	6 weeks
05 May: Duran Duran – The Reflex;	4 weeks
02 Jun: Wham! – Wake Me Up Before You Go-Go;	2 weeks
16 Jun: Frankie Goes To Hollywood – Two Tribes;	9 weeks
18 Aug: George Michael – Careless Whisper;	3 weeks
08 Sep: Stevie Wonder – I Just Called To Say I Love You;	6 weeks
20 Oct: Wham! – Freedom;	3 weeks
10 Nov: Chaka Khan – I Feel For You;	3 weeks
01 Dec: Jim Diamond – I Should Have Known Better;	1 week
08 Dec: Frankie Goes To Hollywood – The Power Of Love;	1 week
15 Dec: Band Aid – Do They Know It's Christmas;	5 weeks

THE US NUMBER ONE SINGLES
OF 1984

07 Jan: Paul McCartney And Michael Jackson – Say Say Say;	2 weeks
21 Jan: Yes – Owner Of A Lonely Heart;	2 weeks
04 Feb: Culture Club – Karma Chameleon;	3 weeks
25 Feb: Van Halen – Jump;	5 weeks
31 Mar: Kenny Loggins – Footloose;	3 weeks
21 Apr: Phil Collins – Against All Odds;	3 weeks
12 May: Lionel Richie – Hello;	2 weeks
26 May: Deniece Williams – Let's Hear It For The Boy;	2 weeks
09 Jun: Cyndi Lauper – Time After Time;	2 weeks
23 Jun: Duran Duran – The Reflex;	2 weeks
07 Jul: Prince – When Doves Cry;	5 weeks
11 Aug: Ray Parker Junior – Ghostbusters;	3 weeks
01 Sep: Tina Turner – What's Love Got To Do With It?;	3 weeks
22 Sep: John Waite – Missing You;	1 week
29 Sep: Prince And The Revolution – Let's Go Crazy;	2 weeks
13 Oct: Stevie Wonder – I Just Called To Say I Love You;	3 weeks
03 Nov: Billy Ocean – Caribbean Queen;	2 weeks
17 Nov: Wham! – Wake Me Up Before You Go-Go;	3 weeks
08 Dec: Daryl Hall & John Oates – Out Of Touch;	2 weeks
22 Dec: Madonna – Like A Virgin;	2 weeks

THE 'UNSUCCESSFUL' UK NUMBER TWO SINGLES OF 1984

14 Jan: Howard Jones – What Is Love;   1 week

04 Feb: Cyndi Lauper – Girls Just Want To Have Fun;   1 week

11 Feb: Queen – Radio Ga Ga;   2 weeks

10 Mar: Kool And The Gang – Joanna/Tonight;   2 weeks

31 Mar: The Weather Girls – It's Raining Men;   1 week

07 Apr: Shakin' Stevens – A Love Worth Waiting For;   2 weeks

21 Apr: The Thompson Twins – You Take Me Up;   1 week

28 Apr: Phil Collins – Against All Odds;   3 weeks

19 May: The Pointer Sisters – Automatic;   2 weeks

02 Jun: Deniece Williams – Let's Hear It For The Boy;   2 weeks

30 Jun: Nik Kershaw – I Won't Let The Sun Go Down On Me;   1 week

21 Jul: Neil – Hole In My Shoe;   3 weeks

18 Aug: Black Lace – Agadoo;   2 weeks

22 Sep: Ray Parker Junior – Ghostbusters;   3 weeks

13 Oct: Culture Club – The War Song;   1 week

27 Oct: Paul McCartney – No More Lonely Nights;   1 week

17 Nov: Duran Duran – Wild Boys;   1 week

15 Dec: Wham! – Last Christmas/Everything She Wants;   5 weeks

THE 'UNSUCCESSFUL' US NUMBER TWO SINGLES OF 1984

11 Feb: Kool And The Gang – Joanna/Tonight

03 Mar: Nena – 99 Luftballoons

10 Mar: Cyndi Lauper – Girls Just Want To Have Fun

24 Mar: Rockwell – Somebody's Watching Me

30 Jun: Bruce Springsteen – Dancing In The Dark

17 Nov: Prince And The Revolution – Purple Rain

15 Dec: Duran Duran – Wild Boys

NEWS HIGHLIGHTS OF 1984

January 10th: Benazir Bhutto is freed from house arrest in Pakistan.

January 13th: Six people die as hurricane-force winds ravage Britain.

January 29th: Ronald Reagan states he will contest the November election.

February 8th: British peace-keeping troops evacuate war-torn Lebanon.

February 15th: Comedian Tommy Cooper collapses on stage and dies.

February 29th: Pierre Trudeau, Canada's Prime Minister, resigns.

March 1st: Tony Benn wins the by-election in Chesterfield.

March 12th: A national coal miners' strike begins in Britain.

March 14th: Gerry Adams is wounded in an assassination attempt.

April 11th: Chernenko is nominated as leader of the Soviet Union.

April 17th: Police constable Yvonne Fletcher is shot dead in London.

April 27th: Thirty Libyan diplomats are obliged to leave Britain.

May 8th: The Soviet Union announces its boycott of the Olympic Games.

May 29th: Police and miners clash at Orgreave coking plant.

May 30th: Arthur Scargill is arrested following the Orgreave riot.

June 2nd: South Africa's President Botha pays a visit to London.

June 6th: Indian troops storm into the Sikhs' Golden Temple in Amritsar.

June 22nd: The first Virgin Atlantic flight leaves Gatwick Airport.

July 9th: York Minster is devastated by a fire.

July 12th: Robert Maxwell buys the Mirror Newspaper Group.

July 28th: The Olympic Games begin in Los Angeles.

August 6th: Soviet dissident, Andrei Sakharov, ends his hunger strike.

August 13th: England lose a fifth successive test to the West Indies.

August 21st: Almost one million Filipinos protest against President Marcos.

September 14th: Shimon Peres becomes Israel's new Prime Minister.

September 15th: Princess Diana gives birth to a second son.

September 28th: The High Court decrees the miners' strike to be unlawful.

October 10th: Arthur Scargill is fined for contempt of court.

October 12th: A bomb attempt to kill Mrs Thatcher narrowly fails.

October 30th: The dead body of Father Popieluszko is discovered.

November 5th: Eight hundred British coal miners return to work.

November 6th: President Ronald Reagan is emphatically re-elected.

November 20th: Shares are offered in British Telecom.

December 10th: Bishop Desmond Tutu is awarded the Nobel Peace Prize.

December 19th: Ted Hughes is appointed as the new Poet Laureate.

December 29th: Rajiv Gandhi emphatically wins the Indian election.

SPORT IN 1984

English Division One football champions: Liverpool; runners-up: Southampton

English FA Cup final: Everton 2 Watford 0

English League Cup Final: Liverpool 1 Everton 0 (in a replay)

Scottish Division One football champions: Aberdeen; runners-up: Glasgow Celtic

Scottish FA Cup final: Aberdeen 2 Glasgow Celtic 1 (after extra time)

Scottish League Cup final: Glasgow Rangers 3 Glasgow Celtic 2 (after extra time)

Irish League football champions: Linfield; Irish Cup final: Ballymena United 4 Carrick Rangers 1

League Of Ireland football champions: Shamrock Rovers; cup winners: UCD

European Cup final: Liverpool beat Roma on penalties; 1–1 after extra time

European Cup-Winners' Cup final: Juventus 2 FC Porto 1

UEFA Cup final: Tottenham Hotspur beat Anderlecht 4–3 on penalties; 2–2 on aggregate

English county cricket champions: Essex

Five Nations' rugby union champions: Scotland (the 'grand slam')

Formula One world drivers' champion: Niki Lauda (Austria) in a McLaren car

Gaelic football All-Ireland champions: Kerry; runners-up: Dublin

British Open golf champion: Seve Ballesteros (at St. Andrews)

US Masters golf champion: Ben Crenshaw

US Open golf champion: Fuzzy Zoeller

USPGA golf champion: Lee Trevino

Rugby league Challenge Cup final: Widnes 19 Wigan 6

Wimbledon men's singles tennis final: J McEnroe beat J Connors 6–1, 6–1, 6–2

Wimbledon ladies' singles tennis final: M Navratilova beat C Evert 7–6, 6–2

World snooker final: Steve Davis (England) beat Jimmy White (England) 18–16

The Aintree Grand National steeplechase winner: Hallo Dandy; price 13–1

The Epsom Derby winner: Secreto; jockey – Christy Roche; price 14–1

European Championship final: France 2 Spain 0 (in Paris)

1984's BUCKET-KICKERS

January 20th: Johnny Weissmuller (US actor); aged 79

February 9th: Yuri Andropov (Soviet statesman); aged 69

March 1st: Jackie Coogan (US actor); aged 69

March 5th: Tito Gobbi (Italian singer); aged 68

April 1st: Marvin Gaye (US singer); aged 44

April 5th: Sir Arthur Travers 'Bomber' Harris (British airman); aged 91

April 17th: General Mark Clark (US soldier); aged 87

April 26th: William 'Count' Basie (US bandleader); aged 79

May 4th: Diana Dors (British actress); aged 52

May 8th: Lila Bel Wallace (US publisher); aged 94

May 19th: Sir John Betjeman (British poet); aged 78

May 28th: Eric Morecambe (British comedian); aged 58

June 11th: Enrico Berlinguer (Italian statesman); aged 62

June 22nd: Joseph Losey (US director); aged 75

June 30th: Lillian Hellman (US author); aged 77

July 20th: James F.Fixx (US author); aged 52

July 27th: James Mason (British actress); aged 75

August 5th: Richard Burton (British actor); aged 58

August 14th: John Boynton Priestley (British author); aged 89

August 25th: Truman Capote (US author); aged 59

October 12th: Sir Anthony George Berry (British politician); aged 59

October 19th: Father Jerzy Popieluszko (Polish priest); aged 37

October 21st: Francois Truffaut (French director); aged 52

October 31st: Indira Gandhi (Indian Premier); aged 66

December 28th: Sam Peckinpah (US director); aged 59

The song of the month for January 1985

**I Know Him So Well by Elaine Paige And Barbara Dickson
(peak chart position: No.1)**

This Anglo-Scottish duet were responsible for the second-biggest selling single in the British chart in 1985. Their admirable effort had its origins in the West End musical, called 'Chess'. The composers were none other than Tim Rice and Abba's songwriting duo, Bjorn Ulvaeus and Benny Andersson, whose songwriting royalties were boosted by this tune's four week sojourn at the top of the UK pop summit.

The song of the month for February 1985

How Soon Is Now? by The Smiths (peak chart position: No.24)

Morrissey was at his melancholy best with this tour de force which had originally featured on the group's 'Hatful Of Hollow' long player. 'How Soon Is Now' was hardly happy-go-lucky chart material but the Smiths had accumulated a cult following that compensated for a lack of radio airplay. This opus included such joyous lines as:"You shut your mouth/How can you say I go about things the wrong way/I am human and I need to be loved."

The song of the month for March 1985

Easy Lover by Philip Bailey With Phil Collins (peak chart position: No.1)

Philip Bailey's outstanding voice had decorated many successful efforts from Earth, Wind & Fire, but this Transatlantic collaboration with Phil Collins yielded him his only British chart-topper. Collins, a percussion man as well as a vocalist was experiencing further commercial success outside of his Genesis projects. This fine dance song failed narrowly to also climb to the peak of the Billboard Hot 100 in the United States.

The song of the month for April 1985
We Are The World by USA For Africa (peak chart position: No 1)

Not to be outdone by the heartwarming response to Band Aid's Christmas smash hit, a plethora of American singing stars belatedly followed in the footsteps of Bob Geldof and Midge Ure and issued their own fundraising single. Featuring the likes of Michael Jackson, Cyndi Lauper, and Huey Lewis, this superstar gathering not surprisingly found favour with music lovers on both sides of the Atlantic, and all in a worthwhile cause.

The song of the month for May 1985
19 by Paul Hardcastle (peak chart position: No.1)

Paul Hardcastle may not have provided the vocals but his keyboard wizardry underpinned this most unusual hit single. For the uninitiated, this song dwelt on the fact that the average age of the American combat soldier in the Vietnam military debacle was nineteen. The accompanying video footage of the world's first televised conflict reinforced this. Hardcastle was also the author of the 'Top Of The Pops' new signature tune.

The song of the month for June 1985
Crazy For You by Madonna (peak chart position: No.2)

Louise Madonna Ciccone had quickly joined the megastar league with several terrific pop hits in quick succession. However, 'Crazy For You' was something of a departure for the American icon as she excelled at a slow, romantic number that demonstrated her adaptability in terms of subject matter. Although this fine single was soon eclipsed by the chart-topping 'Into The Groove', it remains one of the best love songs of the 1980s.

The song of the month for July 1985

There Must Be An Angel by Eurythmics (peak chart position: No.1)

The Eurythmics enjoyed their only week at the summit of the British hit parade courtesy of the radio-friendly 'There Must Be An Angel', featuring the harmonica of the
great Stevie Wonder. Annie and Dave had already managed to savour chart-topping
glory in the United States with 'Sweet Dreams (Are Made Of This)' but this tune
represented their peak, although they followed up with the admirable 'Sisters Are
Doin' It For Themselves.'

The song of the month for August 1985

Running Up That Hill by Kate Bush (peak chart position: No.3)

Kate Bush re-appeared on the airwaves with a vengeance with a number of impressive
singles that reminded everyone of her unique talent. 'Running Up That Hill' ran up
the British and even American hit lists thanks to a memorable double drum sound to
this dark piece. Bush had been absent from the public domain since she issued 'The
Dreaming' album in 1982. 'Running Up That Hill' was a welcome return for the south
London prodigy.

The song of the month for September 1985

Something About You by Level 42 (peak chart position: No.6)

There was certainly something about this superb pop song which appealed to the
music-buying public, as Mark King and his team stayed on the Top 75 for a note-
worthy seventeen weeks. 'Something About You' is something which merits inclusion
on any 'eighties compilation disc. The keyboards, guitar and vocals all join ranks to
cultivate a feel-good track. Level 42 released several decent singles but this was surely
their best effort.

The song of the month for October 1985
Uncle Sam by Madness (peak chart position: No.21)

Now a sextet, Madness were experiencing something of an identity crisis as the decade unfolded. They perhaps felt they could only project their nutty image for so long, and they were keen to record music which was a bit more subtle than their early material. Consequently, the group lost some of their charm, yet they still contrived to offer very listenable items. 'Uncle Sam' revealed the band's political leanings as they poked fun at the gung-ho militarist nature of some American citizens. The accompanying video makes for amusing watching.

The song of the month for November 1985
West End Girls by The Pet Shop Boys (peak chart position: No.1)

A new sensation was coming to the surface towards the end of the year as the duo of Neil Tennant and the po-faced Chris Lowe launched a brilliant pop career with the tremendous dance song, 'West End Girls'. This techno-pop classic had to wait until the Yuletide season ran its course before it climbed to the top of the British singles chart in January 1986. From then on, the Pet Shop Boys proceeded to nourish their followers with a constant diet of outstanding and innovative recordings that remain worthy of mention many years later.

The song of the month for December 1985
The Sun Always Shines On T.V. by A-ha (peak chart position: No.1)

A-ha had exploded on to the television screens with a memorable video for 'Take On Me' which switched between animation and 'reality'. Norway's finest musical trio then built on this triumph with another marvellous pop song which topped the UK hit parade in early 1986. Morten Harket and his colleagues were also regarded as pin-up material, but this should not detract from the decent quality of 'The Sun Always Shines On T.V.'

THE TOP 10 BEST SELLING UK SINGLES OF 1985:

1 The Power Of Love by Jennifer Rush

2 I Know Him So Well by Elaine Paige & Barbara Dickson

3 Into The Groove by Madonna

4 19 by Paul Hardcastle

5 Frankie by Sister Sledge

6 Dancing In The Street by David Bowie & Mick Jagger

7 Move Closer by Phyllis Nelson

8 Take On Me by A-Ha

9 A Good Heart by Feargal Sharkey

10 I Want To Know What Love Is by Foreigner

ALBUM OF THE YEAR FOR 1985

Hounds Of Love by Kate Bush (released in September)

Side 1 (Hounds Of Love):

1. Running Up That Hill (A Deal with God); 5:03

2. Hounds of Love; 3:02

3. The Big Sky; 4:41

4. Mother Stands for Comfort; 3:07

5. Cloudbusting; 5:10

Side 2 (The Ninth Wave):

1. And Dream of Sheep; 2:45

2. Under Ice; 2:21

3. Waking the Witch; 4:18

4. Watching You Without Me; 4:06

5. Jig of Life; 4:04

6. Hello Earth; 6:13

7. The Morning Fog; 2:34

Kate Bush emerged from hibernation with an album that even exceeded the kudos that she had accumulated from her four previous admirable efforts. This new project was divided into a side one of commercially appealing chart material items while the reverse side focused on the nightmare scenario of drowning. Bush remained her own woman. She wrote and recorded what she wanted when she wanted. Her single-minded approach paid off handsomely here. Even Uncle Sam warmed to 'Running Up That Hill', although the wondrous title track is at least equally deserving of acclaim. 'Cloudbusting' featured the venerable Donald Sutherland in the video and it is difficult not to be swept along on the wave of ecstasy that Kate emotes at the song's joyful conclusion. 'Hounds Of Love' is quirky, just like its author, but it remains hugely listenable.

THE UK NUMBER ONE ALBUMS
OF 1985

19 Jan: Alison Moyet – Alf;	1 week
26 Jan: Foreigner – Agent Provocateur;	3 weeks
16 Feb: Bruce Springsteen – Born In The U.S.A.;	1 week
23 Feb: The Smiths – Meat Is Murder;	1 week
02 Mar: Phil Collins – No Jacket Required;	5 weeks
06 Apr: Paul Young – The Secret Of Association;	1 week
13 Apr: Various artist comp. (CBS/WEA) –	
The Hits Album 2/The Hits Tape 2;	6 weeks
25 May: Dire Straits – Brothers In Arms;	2 weeks
08 Jun: Style Council – Our Favourite Shop;	1 week
15 Jun: Bryan Ferry – Boys And Girls;	2 weeks
29 Jun: Marillion – Misplaced Childhood;	1 week
06 Jul: Bruce Springsteen – Born In The U.S.A.;	4 weeks
03 Aug: Dire Straits – Brothers In Arms;	2 weeks
17 Aug: Various artist comp. (Virgin/EMI) –	
Now That's What I Call Music 5;	5 weeks
21 Sep: Madonna – Like A Virgin;	1 week
28 Sep: Kate Bush – Hounds Of Love;	2 weeks
12 Oct: Madonna – Like A Virgin;	1 week
19 Oct: Kate Bush – Hounds Of Love;	1 week
26 Oct: George Benson – The Love Songs;	1 week
02 Nov: Simple Minds – Once Upon A Time;	1 week
09 Nov: George Benson – The Love Songs;	1 week
16 Nov: Sade – Promise;	2 weeks
30 Nov: Various artist comp. (Telstar) – The Greatest Hits Of 1985;	1 week
07 Dec: Various artist comp. (Virgin/EMI) –	
Now That's What I Call Music 6;	2 weeks
21 Dec: Various artist comp. (Virgin/EMI) –	
Now – The Christmas Album;	2 weeks

THE US NUMBER ONE ALBUMS OF 1985

05 Jan: Prince And The Revolution – Purple Rain;	2 weeks
19 Jan: Bruce Springsteen – Born In The U.S.A.;	3 weeks
09 Feb: Madonna – Like A Virgin;	3 weeks
02 Mar: Wham! – Make It Big;	3 weeks
23 Mar: John Fogerty – Centerfold;	2 weeks
30 Mar: Phil Collins – No Jacket Required;	4 weeks
27 Apr: USA For Africa – We Are The World;	3 weeks
18 May: Phil Collins – No Jacket Required;	2 weeks
01 Jun: Prince And The Revolution – Around The World In A Day;	3 weeks
22 Jun: Soundtrack – Beverly Hills Cop;	2 weeks
06 Jul: Phil Collins – No Jacket Required;	1 week
13 Jul: Tears For Fears – Songs From The Big Chair;	4 weeks
10 Aug: Bryan Adams – Reckless;	2 weeks
24 Aug: Tears For Fears – Songs From The Big Chair;	1 week
31 Aug: Dire Straits – Brothers In Arms;	9 weeks
02 Nov: Soundtrack – Miami Vice;	7 weeks
21 Dec: Heart – Heart;	1 week
28 Dec: Soundtrack – Miami Vice	

THE UK NUMBER ONE SINGLES
OF 1985

19 Jan: Foreigner – I Want To Know What Love Is;	3 weeks
09 Feb: Elaine Paige & Barbara Dickson – I Know Him So Well;	4 weeks
09 Mar: Dead Or Alive – You Spin Me Round (Like A Record);	2 weeks
23 Mar: Philip Bailey & Phil Collins – Easy Lover;	4 weeks
20 Apr: USA For Africa – We Are The World;	2 weeks
04 May: Phillis Nelson – Move Closer;	1 week
11 May: Paul Hardcastle – 19;	5 weeks
15 Jun: The Crowd – You'll Never Walk Alone;	2 weeks
29 Jun: Sister Sledge – Frankie;	4 weeks
27 Jul: Eurythmics – There Must Be An Angel;	1 week
03 Aug: Madonna – Into The Groove;	4 weeks
31 Aug: UB40 & Chrissie Hynde – I Got You Babe;	1 week
07 Sep: David Bowie & Mick Jagger – Dancing in the Streets;	4 weeks
05 Oct: Midge Ure – If I Was;	1 week
12 Oct: Jennifer Rush – The Power Of Love;	5 weeks
16 Nov: Feargal Sharkey – A Good Heart;	2 weeks
30 Nov: Wham! – I'm Your Man;	2 weeks
14 Dec: Whitney Houston – Saving All My Love For You;	2 weeks
28 Dec: Shakin' Stevens – Merry Christmas Everyone;	2 weeks

THE US NUMBER ONE SINGLES OF 1985

05 Jan: Madonna – Like A Virgin;	4 weeks
02 Feb: Foreigner – I Want To Know What Love Is;	2 weeks
16 Feb: Wham! featuring George Michael – Careless Whisper;	3 weeks
09 Mar: REO Speedwagon – Can't Fight This Feeling;	3 weeks
30 Mar: Phil Collins – One More Night;	2 weeks
13 Apr: USA For Africa – We Are The World;	4 weeks
11 May: Madonna – Crazy For You;	1 week
18 May: Simple Minds – Don't You (Forget About Me);	1 week
25 May: Wham! – Everything She Wants;	2 weeks
08 Jun: Tears For Fears – Everybody Wants To Rule The World;	2 weeks
22 Jun: Bryan Adams – Heaven;	2 weeks
06 Jul: Phil Collins – Sussudio;	1 week
13 Jul: Duran Duran – A View To A Kill;	2 weeks
27 Jul: Paul Young – Everytime You Go Away;	1 week
03 Aug: Tears For Fears – Shout;	3 weeks
24 Aug: Huey Lewis And The News – The Power Of Love;	2 weeks
07 Sep: John Parr – St. Elmo's Fire (Man In Motion);	2 weeks
21 Sep: Dire Straits – Money For Nothing;	3 weeks
12 Oct: Ready For The World – Oh Sheila;	1 week
19 Oct: A-ha – Take On Me;	1 week
26 Oct: Whitney Houston – Saving All My Love For You;	1 week
02 Nov: Stevie Wonder – Part-Time Lover;	1 week
09 Nov: Jan Hammer – Miami Vice Theme;	1 week
16 Nov: Starship – We Built This City;	2 weeks
30 Nov: Phil Collins & Marilyn Martin – Separate Lives;	1 week
07 Dec: Mr. Mister – Broken Wings;	2 weeks
21 Dec: Lionel Richie – Say You, Say Me;	2 weeks

THE 'UNSUCCESSFUL' UK NUMBER TWO SINGLES OF 1985

26 Jan: Prince And The Revolution – 1999;   1 week

09 Feb: King – Love And Pride;   3 weeks

23 Mar: Alison Moyet – That Ole Devil Called Love;   2 weeks

06 Apr: Frankie Goes To Hollywood – Welcome To The Pleasuredome;   2 weeks

20 Apr: Tears For Fears – Everybody Wants To Rule The World;   2 weeks

25 May: Duran Duran – A View To A Kill;   3 weeks

15 Jun: Marillion – Kayleigh;   1 week

29 Jun: Madonna – Crazy For You;   1 week

06 Jul: Harold Faltermeyer – Axel F;   3 weeks

17 Aug: Madonna – Holiday;   1 week

14 Sep: Bonnie Tyler – Holding Out For A Hero;   3 weeks

26 Oct: A-ha – Take On Me;   3 weeks

THE 'UNSUCCESSFUL' US NUMBER TWO SINGLES OF 1985

12 Jan: Jack Wagner – All I Need

02 Feb: Philip Bailey With Phil Collins – Easy Lover

23 Feb: Billy Ocean – Loverboy

16 Mar: Glenn Frey – The Heat Is On

23 Mar: Madonna – Material Girl

20 Jul: Prince And The Revolution – Raspberry Beret

14 Sep: Tina Turner – We Don't Need Another Hero

21 Sep: Kool And The Gang – Cherish

16 Nov: Glenn Frey – You Belong To The City

28 Dec: Eddie Murphy – Party All The Time

NEWS HIGHLIGHTS OF 1985

January 14th: Fowler and Gatting hit double centuries against India.
January 16th: The Sultan of Brunei buys the Dorchester Hotel.
January 26th: The Pope begins a tour of South America.
February 4th: Spain ends its sixteen-year siege of Gibraltar.
February 20th: Mrs Thatcher addresses the American Congress.
February 28th: Newry police station suffers a mortar attack.
March 3rd: The National Union of Mineworkers ends its strike.
March 11th: Mikhail Gorbachev is chosen as the new Russian leader.
March 11th: The Al-Fayeds win control of the House of Fraser.
April 7th: Wham! arrive in China to perform two concerts.
April 8th: Rupert Murdoch invests in Twentieth-Century Fox.
April 30th: Ronald Reagan proposes a trade embargo on Nicaragua.
May 8th: President Reagan addresses the European Parliament.
May 11th: Fire sweeps through Bradford City's Valley Parade ground.
May 29th: Rioting occurs at the European Cup Final in Brussels.
June 2nd: English football clubs are banned from Europe "indefinitely".
June 8th: Barry McGuigan becomes world featherweight champion.
June 23rd: An Air India flight explodes and crashes into the sea.
July 10th: Greenpeace's Rainbow Warrior suffers two explosions.
July 13th: Live Aid is staged to raise funds for famine relief.
July 27th: Uganda's President Obote is deposed in a coup.
August 8th: The Pope begins a seven-nation tour of Africa.
August 22nd: An aeroplane catches fire at Manchester Airport.
August 26th: Zola Budd breaks the 5,000 metres world record.
September 2nd: Douglas Hurd is appointed as the Home Secretary.
September 23rd: Rupert Murdoch buys the rest of 20th Century Fox.
September 29th: Rioting breaks out in Brixton.
October 1st: Rioting extends to Peckham and Toxteth.
October 19th: The Union of Democratic Mineworkers is formed.
October 21st: Thirteen die in Britain's worst motorway accident.
November 15th: The Anglo-Irish Agreement is signed.
November 19th: Gorbachev and Reagan meet in Geneva for talks.
November 27th: Gorbachev says that the meeting was "a positive start."
December 8th: Princess Anne appeals for famine relief for Sudan.
December 11th: Loyalists protest against the Anglo-Irish Agreement.
December 30th: Rome and Vienna airports suffer terrorist attacks.

SPORT IN 1985

English Division One football champions: Everton; runners-up: Liverpool

English FA Cup final: Manchester United 1 Everton 0 (after extra time)

English League Cup Final: Norwich City 1 Sunderland 0

Scottish Premier League football champions: Aberdeen; runners-up: Glasgow Celtic

Scottish FA Cup final: Glasgow Celtic 2 Dundee United 1

Scottish League Cup final: Glasgow Rangers 1 Dundee United 0

Irish League football champions: Linfield; Irish Cup final: Glentoran 1 Linfield 0 (in a replay)

League Of Ireland football champions: Shamrock Rovers; cup winners: Shamrock Rovers

European Cup final: Juventus 1 Liverpool 0

European Cup-Winners' Cup final: Everton 3 Rapid Vienna 1

UEFA Cup final: Real Madrid beat Videoton 3–1 on aggregate

English county cricket champions: Middlesex

Five Nations' rugby union champions: Ireland (the 'triple crown')

Formula One world drivers' champion: Alain Prost (France) in a McLaren car

Gaelic football All-Ireland champions: Kerry; runners-up: Dublin

British Open golf champion: Sandy Lyle (at Royal St. George's)

US Masters golf champion: Bernhard Langer

US Open golf champion: Andy North

USPGA golf champion: Hubert Green

Rugby league Challenge Cup final: Wigan 28 Hull 24

Wimbledon men's singles tennis final: B Becker beat K Curren 6–3, 6–7, 7–6, 6–4

Wimbledon ladies' singles tennis final: M Navratilova beat C Evert 4–6, 6–3, 6–2

World snooker final: Dennis Taylor (Northern Ireland) beat Steve Davis (England) 18–17

The Aintree Grand National steeplechase winner: Last Suspect; price 50–1

The Epsom Derby winner: Slip Anchor; jockey – Steve Cauthen; price 9–4F

The Ryder Cup: Europe 16.5 The United States Of America 11.5

1985's BUCKET-KICKERS

January 16th: Sir Robert Mayer (British philanthropist); aged 105

January 26th: Mark James Walter Cameron (British journalist); aged 73

January 26th: William David Ormsby Gore (British diplomat); aged 66

March 10th: Konstantin Chernenko (Soviet statesman); aged 73

March 21st: Sir Michael Scudamore Redgrave (British actor); aged 77

March 28th: Marc Chagall (French painter); aged 97

April 11th: Enver Hoxha (Albanian dictator); aged 76

May 28th: Francis Roy Plomley (British broadcaster); aged 71

June 2nd: George Alfred Brown (ex-British Foreign Secretary); aged 70

September 17th: Laura Ashley (British designer); aged 60

October 2nd: Rock Hudson (US actor); aged 59

October 6th: Keith Henry Blakelock (British policeman); aged 40

October 10th: Yul Brynner (US actor); aged 65

October 10th: Orson Welles (US actor); aged 70

October 25th: Gary Holton (British actor); aged 33

November 17th: Lon Nol (Cambodian leader); aged 72

December 2nd: Philip Arthur Larkin (British poet); aged 63

December 7th: Robert Ranke Graves (British author); aged 90

The song of the month for January 1986

Chain Reaction by Diana Ross (peak chart position: No.1)

The great Diana Ross re-visited the British pop summit for the first time in more than fourteen years with the excellent 'Chain Reaction'. In the intervening decade and a half the talented chanteuse had unleashed a whole host of wondrous love songs and dance tunes for music lovers to feast themselves on, yet it took the likeable 'Chain Reaction' to land the popular lady back on once-familiar territory. 'Chain Reaction' was penned by the Bee Gees who also provided vocals.

The song of the month for February 1986

Eloise by The Damned (peak chart position: No.3)

The Damned sold their punk souls for a slice of pop fame when they abandoned their usual repertoire in favour of an excellent cover version of Barry Ryan's 'Eloise'. The single narrowly missed out on a British Number One, but it was obviously one of the highlights of 1986, albeit from an unlikely source. Quite clearly Rat Scabies and the gang had bills to pay, hence their surprising choice of recording. 'Eloise' had previously climbed to Number 2 back in 1968.

The song of the month for March 1986

A Kind Of Magic by Queen (peak chart position: No.3)

After the success of 'The Works', Queen were once more parading an exciting new array of tunes, that comprised the 'A Kind Of Magic' album. The long player was magical by name and magical by nature, with some of the songs forming the soundtrack to the new 'Highlander' movie. The singles from this LP were of the highest order, namely the poignant 'Who Wants To Live Forever' and the Top 10 hit 'One Vision'. However Roger Taylor's 'A Kind Of Magic' is in a class of its own.

The song of the month for April 1986

Live To Tell by Madonna (peak chart position: No ?)

Madonna cemented the sensational success of her previous two years with more triumphant forays into the British singles chart in 1986, courtesy of her new 'True Blue' album. Nevertheless my own preference is for the tremendous 'Live To Tell' hit in which our Madge bares her soul and forsakes her customary dance repertoire, confirming that she was more than a one trick pony. As long as she continued to vary her output, Madonna was assured of a sustained chart career.

The song of the month for May 1986

Bigmouth Strikes Again by The Smiths (peak chart position: No.26)

In an exercise of revisionism, the eminent historian Steven Patrick Morrissey made us all aware that Joan Of Arc had actually been the first proud owner of both a walkman and a hearing aid as well as being a temporary scourge of the English. Bigmouth himself, Mr Morrissey, was once more offering his alternate take on that old thing called love, as he sings from the point of view of an apologetic bloke who pleads with his "sweetness" that he was only joking when he said that by rights she "should be bludgeoned" in her bed. It did make a refreshing change from the "I'm lonely without you baby" drivel that usually invaded the charts.

The song of the month for June 1986

Higher Love by Steve Winwood (peak chart position: No.13)

'Sixties legend Stevie Winwood made a welcome return to the upper echelons of the British hit parade with 'Higher Love'. Having previously tasted chart-topping glory with the Spencer Davis Group as a teenage prodigy as well as further success with Traffic , the grown-up Winwood was back in vogue, especially in the United States where this new recording leapt to the peak position of the Billboard Hot 100 listings towards the end of the summer.

The song of the month for July 1986

Every Beat Of My Heart by Rod Stewart (peak chart position: No.2)

Scotland's greatest vocalist was back on the airwaves with another formidable composition, a mere three years after 'Baby Jane' had yielded him his fifth UK chart-topper. 'Every Beat Of My Heart' just failed to become Rod's sixth Number One, but it was a throwback to his seminal 'Sailing' recording as the old mod gets all sentimental about his homeland with the accompaniment of bagpipes and forgets about his fun blondes for a few minutes.

The song of the month for August 1986

Word Up by Cameo (peak chart position: No.3)

Cameo hardly enjoyed a durable career in the world of music but they did make one enormous splash with the dancefloor favourite 'Word Up'. This superb pop song was a welcome inclusion in the British Top Three in the autumn of 1986, and it will perhaps be best remembered for the group's appearances on BBC's 'Top Of The Pops' whereupon the lead singer cheekily displays an outfit that came seriously close to exposing his manhood, though I guess that was his intention.

The song of the month for September 1986

True Colors by Cyndi Lauper (peak chart position: No.12)

'True Colors' is a truly towering piece from the colourful Cyndi Lauper. It perhaps surpasses the very different 'Girls Just Want To Have Fun' as her best recording. Here Miss Lauper shares words of wisdom and encouragement with a beautiful, uplifting track that found favour with American record buyers. Not for the first time, British music lovers took leave of their senses and failed to appreciate this stunning song. A plague on all their houses!

The song of the month for October 1986

Always The Sun by The Stranglers (peak chart position: No 30)

Punk pioneers The Stranglers continued to invade the singles charts at various intervals, but not even the hugely popular 'Golden Brown' can quite compare with the
musical treat that was 'Always The Sun'. Here Hugh and his comrades get all philo-
sophical about the fact that no matter how much life sucks and doesn't go according
to plan, "there's always the sun". This brilliant item also ought to have been embraced
by more record-buyers, but it is still an 'eighties classic.

The song of the month for November 1986

French Kissin' In The USA by Debbie Harry (peak chart position: No.8)

Debbie Harry might have expected to go from strength to strength after the break-up
of Blondie but her initial solo effort 'Backfired' did precisely that and the ageing blonde
bombshell had to jettison her solo career for a while as she nursed her partner Chris
Stein back from a serious bout of ill health. Stein and Harry were eventually back on
top form with the marvellous 'French Kissin' In The USA' which actually represented
their first UK Top Ten hit in almost six barren years.

The song of the month for December 1986

Hymn To Her by The Pretenders (peak chart position: No.8)

Chrissie Hynde survived the double trauma of losing half her band to drug abuse to
re-group and return with the occasional jewel of a recording. The new look Pretenders
sneaked back into the British Top Ten with the commendable 'Hymn To Her'. It was
refreshing for Hynde to have a musical success story to crow about, away from regular
tabloid coverage of her dalliances with the singers Ray Davies of the Kinks, Jim Kerr
of Simple Minds, and then Ali Campbell of UB40.

THE TOP 10 BEST SELLING UK SINGLES OF 1986

1 Don't Leave Me This Way by The Communards

2 Every Loser Wins by Nick Berry

3 I Want To Wake Up With You by Boris Gardiner

4 Living Doll by Cliff Richard & The Young Ones

5 Chain Reaction by Diana Ross

6 Lady In Red by Chris De Burgh

7 When The Going Gets Tough by Billy Ocean

8 Take My Breath Away by Berlin

9 Papa Don't Preach by Madonna

10 So Macho by Sinitta

ALBUM OF THE YEAR FOR 1986

Graceland by Paul Simon (released in August)

Side 1:

1. The Boy In The Bubble; 3:59

2. Graceland; 4:48

3. I Know What I Know; 3:13

4. Gumboots; 2:44

5. Diamonds on the Soles of Her Shoes; 5:45

Side 2:

1. You Can Call Me Al; 4:39

2. Under African Skies; 3:37

3. Homeless; 3:48

4. Crazy Love, Vol.II; 4:18

5. That Was Your Mother; 2:52

6. All Around the World or the Myth of Fingerprints; 3:15

Paul Simon incurred the wrath of the anti-apartheid movement when he recorded his new 'Graceland' project in South Africa, thus defying an international boycott. This was a bit harsh, considering that his album acted as a commercial for (South) African music as he was showcasing the talents of some of the country's most renowned performers. The vocal harmonies of 'Homeless' and 'I Know What I Know' are the obvious examples of that. Furthermore, Simon recruited the likes of Linda Ronstadt for a memorable bout of backing vocals on 'Under African Skies', whilst Phil and Don Everly were drafted in to vocally decorate the outstanding title track. For all the negative reaction in certain quarters, Simon had delivered his most impressive long player since 'Bridge Over Troubled Water' and it certainly found favour with record buyers around the globe. It narrowly defeats 'So' by Peter Gabriel for my choice of the best album of 1986.

THE UK NUMBER ONE ALBUMS
OF 1986

04 Jan: Various artist comp. (Virgin/EMI) –
    Now That's What I Call Music 6;   2 weeks

18 Jan: Dire Straits – Brothers In Arms;   10 weeks

29 Mar: Various artist comp. (CBS/WEA) – Hits 4;   4 weeks

26 Apr: Bryan Ferry & Roxy Music – Street Life – 20 Greatest Hits;   5 weeks

31 May: Peter Gabriel – So;   2 weeks

14 Jun: Queen – A Kind Of Magic;   1 week

21 Jun: Genesis – Invisible Touch;   3 weeks

12 Jul: Madonna – True Blue;   6 weeks

23 Aug: Various artist comp. (Virgin/EMI) –
    Now That's What I Call Music 7;   5 weeks

27 Sep: Five Star – Silk And Steel;   1 week

04 Oct: Paul Simon – Graceland;   5 weeks

08 Nov: The Police – Every Breath You Take – The Singles;   2 weeks

22 Nov: Various artist comp. (CBS/WEA) – Hits 5;   2 weeks

06 Dec: Various artist comp. (EMI/Virgin) –
    Now That's What I Call Music 8;   6 weeks

THE US NUMBER ONE ALBUMS OF 1986

04 Jan: Soundtrack – Miami Vice;	3 weeks
25 Jan: Barbra Streisand – The Broadway Album;	3 weeks
15 Feb: Sade – Promise;	2 weeks
01 Mar: Mr.Mister – Welcome To The Real World;	1 week
08 Mar: Whitney Houston – Whitney Houston;	7 weeks
26 Apr: Van Halen – 5150;	3 weeks
17 May: Whitney Houston – Whitney Houston;	7 weeks
05 Jul: Janet Jackson – Control;	2 weeks
19 Jul: Patti LaBelle – Winner In You;	1 week
26 Jul: Soundtrack – Top Gun;	3 weeks
16 Aug: Madonna – True Blue;	5 weeks
20 Sep: Soundtrack – Top Gun;	1 week
27 Sep: Lionel Richie – Dancing On The Ceiling;	2 weeks
11 Oct: Soundtrack – Top Gun;	1 week
18 Oct: Huey Lewis & The News – Fore!;	1 week
25 Oct: Bon Jovi – Slippery When Wet;	1 week
01 Nov: Boston – Third Stage;	4 weeks
29 Nov: Bruce Springsteen – Live/1975–85;	5 weeks

THE UK NUMBER ONE SINGLES
OF 1986

11 Jan: Pet Shop Boys – West End Girls;	2 weeks
25 Jan: A-ha – The Sun Always Shines On TV;	2 weeks
08 Feb: Billy Ocean – When The Going Gets Tough, The Tough Get Going;	4 weeks
08 Mar: Diana Ross – Chain Reaction;	3 weeks
29 Mar: Cliff Richard & The Young Ones – Living Doll;	3 weeks
19 Apr: George Michael – A Different Corner;	3 weeks
10 May: Falco – Rock Me Amadeus;	1 week
17 May: Spitting Image – The Chicken Song;	3 weeks
07 Jun: Doctor & The Medics – Spirit In The Sky;	3 weeks
28 Jun: Wham! – The Edge Of Heaven;	2 weeks
12 Jul: Madonna – Papa Don't Preach;	3 weeks
02 Aug: Chris de Burgh – The Lady In Red;	3 weeks
23 Aug: Boris Gardiner – I Want To Wake Up With You;	3 weeks
13 Sep: The Communards – Don't Leave Me This Way;	4 weeks
11 Oct: Madonna – True Blue;	1 week
18 Oct: Nick Berry – Every Loser Wins;	3 weeks
08 Nov: Berlin – Take My Breath Away;	4 weeks
06 Dec: Europe – The Final Countdown;	2 weeks
20 Dec: The Housemartins – Caravan Of Love;	1 week
27 Dec: Jackie Wilson – Reet Petite:	4 weeks

THE US NUMBER ONE SINGLES OF 1986

04 Jan: Lionel Richie – Say You, Say Me;	2 weeks
18 Jan: Dionne And Friends – That's What Friends Are For;	4 weeks
15 Feb: Whitney Houston – How Will I Know;	2 weeks
1 Mar: Mr. Mister – Kyrie;	2 weeks
15 Mar: Starship – Sara;	1 week
22 Mar: Heart – These Dreams;	1 week
29 Mar: Falco – Rock Me Amadeus;	3 weeks
19 Apr: Prince And The Revolution – Kiss;	2 weeks
03 May: Robert Palmer – Addicted To Love;	1 week
10 May: The Pet Shop Boys – West End Girls;	1 week
17 May: Whitney Houston – Greatest Love Of All;	3 weeks
07 Jun: Madonna – Live To Tell;	1 week
14 Jun: Patti LaBelle & Michael McDonald – On My Own;	3 weeks
05 Jul: Billy Ocean – There'll Be Sad Songs (To Make You Cry);	1 week
12 Jul: Simply Red – Holding Back The Years;	1 week
19 Jul: Genesis – Invisible Touch;	1 week
26 Jul: Peter Gabriel – Sledgehammer;	1 week
02 Aug: Peter Cetera – Glory Of Love;	2 weeks
16 Aug: Madonna – Papa Don't Preach;	2 weeks
30 Aug: Steve Winwood – Higher Love;	1 week
06 Sep: Bananarama – Venus;	1 week
13 Sep: Berlin – Take My Breath Away;	1 week
20 Sep: Huey Lewis & The News – Stuck With You;	3 weeks
11 Oct: Janet Jackson – When I Think Of You;	2 weeks
25 Oct: Cyndi Lauper – True Colors;	2 weeks
08 Nov: Boston – Amanda;	2 weeks
22 Nov: Human League – Human;	1 week
29 Nov: Bon Jovi – You Give Love A Bad Name;	1 week
06 Dec: Peter Cetera With Amy Grant – The Next Time I Fall;	1 week
13 Dec: Bruce Hornsby & The Range – The Way It Is;	1 week
20 Dec: The Bangles – Walk Like An Egyptian;	2 weeks

THE 'UNSUCCESSFUL' UK NUMBER TWO SINGLES OF 1986

25 Jan: Dire Straits – Walk Of Life;   1 week

01 Feb: Nana Mouskouri – Only Love;   1 week

15 Feb: Madonna – Borderline;   1 week

22 Feb: Su Pollard – Starting Together;   1 week

15 Mar: The Bangles – Manic Monday;   1 week

22 Mar: David Bowie – Absolute Beginners;   1 week

05 Apr: Sam Cooke – Wonderful World;   1 week

10 May: Madonna – Live To Tell;   1 week

17 May: Patti LaBelle & Michael McDonald – On My Own;   3 weeks

07 Jun: Simply Red – Holding Back The Years;   2 weeks

28 Jun: Nu Shooz – I Can't Wait;   1 week

19 Jul: Rod Stewart – Every Beat Of My Heart;   1 week

09 Aug: Sinitta – So Macho;   2 weeks

20 Sep: Jermaine Stewart – We Don't Have To Take Our Clothes Off;   2 weeks

04 Oct: Five Star – Rain Or Shine;   2 weeks

01 Nov: Status Quo – In The Army Now;   1 week

15 Nov: Kim Wilde – You Keep Me Hangin' On;   2 weeks

13 Dec: Erasure – Sometimes;   2 weeks

THE 'UNSUCCESSFUL' US NUMBER TWO SINGLES OF 1986

01 Feb: Survivor – Burning Heart

15 Feb: Billy Ocean – When The Going Gets Tough, The Tough Get Going

05 Apr: John Cougar Mellencamp – Rock In The USA

19 Apr: The Bangles – Manic Monday

26 Jul: Kenny Loggins – Danger Zone

13 Sep: Lionel Richie – Dancing On The Ceiling

27 Sep: Gloria Loring And Carl Anderson – Friends And Lovers

11 Oct: Glass Tiger – Don't Forget Me When I'm Gone

18 Oct: Tina Turner – Typical Male

08 Nov: Robert Palmer – I Didn't Mean To Turn You On

27 Dec: Wang Chung – Everybody Have Fun Tonight

NEWS HIGHLIGHTS OF 1986

January 9th: Michael Heseltine resigns from the Thatcher government.
January 24th: Leon Brittan also resigns, a result of the Westland Affair.
January 28th: The American space shuttle Challenger explodes into flames.
February 7th: The dictator 'Baby Doc' Duvalier flees from Haiti.
February 12th: Thatcher and Mitterand sign a Channel Tunnel agreement.
February 25th: President Marcos is ousted by Corazon Aquino in Manila.
March 16th: The Front Nationale makes gains in France's general election.
March 19th: The engagement of Prince Andrew and 'Fergie' is announced.
March 20th: Jacques Chirac becomes Prime Minister of France.
April 7th: Sir Clive Sinclair sells his computer business to Alan Sugar.
April 10th: Benazir Bhutto returns to Pakistan, demanding free elections.
April 15th: The Americans launch an air strike against Tripoli in Libya.
May 8th: The Labour Party make gains in British local council elections.
May 21st: Ken Baker is appointed Secretary of State for Education.
May 25th: Thirty million run the 'Race Against Time' for famine relief.
June 8th: Dr Kurt Waldheim is elected as President of Austria.
June 12th: South Africa declares a state of emergency.
June 22nd: Maradona's hand ensures England's exit from the World Cup.
July 23rd: Prince Andrew and Sarah Ferguson get married.
July 27th: American cyclist Greg Lemond wins the Tour de France.
July 29th: Culture Club's Boy George is convicted of possessing heroin.
August 10th: An earthquake occurs in San Salvador.
August 14th: Benazir Bhutto is arrested in Karachi.
August 31st: Two aeroplanes collide over Los Angeles.
September 7th: Desmond Tutu is enthroned as Archbishop of Cape Town.
September 8th: Nissan opens a car factory in Sunderland.
September 28th: Lloyd Honeyghan becomes world boxing champion.
October 20th: Yitzhak Shamir becomes Prime Minister of Israel.
October 26th: Jeffrey Archer resigns as the Conservatives' deputy chairman.
October 27th: The London Stock Exchange goes all computerised.
November 4th: The Democrats win control of the American Senate.
November 20th: Police search Saddleworth Moor for two missing children.
November 22nd: Mike Tyson becomes world heavyweight boxing champion.
December 17th: John De Lorean is acquitted of embezzlement.
December 19th: John Stalker resigns from the police force.
December 28th:England retain the Ashes after victory in a Melbourne test.

SPORT IN 1986

English Division One football champions: Liverpool; runners-up: Everton

English FA Cup final: Liverpool 3 Everton 1

English League Cup Final: Oxford United 3 Queen's Park Rangers 0

Scottish Premier League football champions: Glasgow Celtic; runners-up: Heart Of Midlothian

Scottish FA Cup final: Aberdeen 3 Heart Of Midlothian 0

Scottish League Cup final: Aberdeen 3 Hibernian 0

Irish League football champions: Linfield; Irish Cup final: Glentoran 2 Coleraine 1

League Of Ireland football champions: Shamrock Rovers; cup winners: Shamrock Rovers

European Cup final: Steaua Bucuresti beat Barcelona on penalties; 0–0 after extra time

European Cup-Winners' Cup final: Dinamo Kiev 3 Atletico Madrid 0

UEFA Cup final: Real Madrid beat FC Koln 5–3 on aggregate

English county cricket champions: Essex

Five Nations' rugby union champions: France and Scotland (both 6 points)

Formula One world drivers' champion: Alain Prost (France) in a McLaren car

Gaelic football All-Ireland champions: Kerry; runners-up: Tyrone

British Open golf champion: Greg Norman (at Turnberry)

US Masters golf champion: Jack Nicklaus

US Open golf champion: Raymond Floyd

USPGA golf champion: Bob Tway

Rugby league Challenge Cup final: Castleford 15 Hull Kingston Rovers 14

Wimbledon men's singles tennis final: B Becker beat I Lendl 6–4, 6–3, 7–5

Wimbledon ladies' singles tennis final: M Navratilova beat H Mandlikova 7–6, 6–3

World snooker final: Joe Johnson (England) beat Steve Davis (England) 18–12

The Aintree Grand National steeplechase winner: West Tip; price 15–2

The Epsom Derby winner: Shahrastani; jockey – Walter Swinburn; price 11–2

Football World Cup final: Argentina 3 West Germany 2 (in Mexico City)

1986's BUCKET-KICKERS

January 4th: Christopher Isherwood (US novelist); aged 81

January 4th: Philip Parris Lynott (British musician); aged 36

February 28th: Olof Palme (Sweden's Premier); aged 59

March 14th: Sir Huw Pyrs Wheldon (British author); aged 69

March 17th: Lieutenant-General Sir John Bagot Glubb (British soldier); aged 88

March 30th: James Cagney (US actor); aged 86

April 14th: Simone de Beauvoir (French author); aged 78

April 15th: Jean Genet (French playwright); aged 75

April 23rd: Jim Laker (British cricketer); aged 64

April 23rd: Otto Preminger (US director); aged 79

April 24th: Duchess Wallis Warfield Simpson; aged 89

May 9th: Tensing Norgay (Nepalese mountaineer); aged 71

June 3rd: Dame Anna Neagle (British actress); aged 81

June 13th: Benny Goodman (US clarinettist); aged 77

June 14th:Jorge Luis Borges (Argentine author); aged 86

July 26th: Averell Harriman (US politician); aged 94

August 31st: Henry Moore (British sculptor); aged 88

October 16th: Arthur Grumiaux (Belgian violinist); aged 65

November 8th: Vyacheslav Molotov (Soviet statesman); aged 96

November 29th: Cary Grant (US actor); aged 82

December 29th: Maurice Harold Macmillan (ex-British Premier); aged 92

The song of the month for January 1987

I Knew You Were Waiting (For Me) by Aretha Franklin & George Michael (peak chart position: No.1)

George Michael, having previously collaborated with Andrew Ridgeley would proceed over the course of the next decade to join forces with such slightly more talented acts as Elton John and Queen, and on this notable occasion with the 'Queen of soul', Aretha Franklin. Remarkably, this was the only chart-topping triumph for Aretha but this Transatlantic smash hit is undoubtedly one of the great Number Ones of the 'eighties.

The song of the month for February 1987

Shoplifters Of The World Unite by The Smiths (peak chart position: No.12)

The polar opposites of Morrissey and guitarist Johnny Marr have accurately been held up as Britain's most important songwriting duo since Lennon and McCartney. The latest poetry in motion from their factory of hits was the black humour of 'Shoplifters Of The World Unite' in which Morrissey confesses that his "only weakness is a listed crime." Regrettably, Morrissey and Marr would soon sue for divorce due to irreconcilable differences.

The song of the month for March 1987

Mothers Of The Disappeared by U2 (not released as a single)

U2 had come a long way since their early punk leanings and their raw rock. Now the Edge, with the considerable help of ace producers Daniel Lanois and Brian Eno, was constructing sounds and imagery that took rock onto a new plateau. Bono was now in the business of raising awareness of serious issues rather than reverting to the standards of female conquests and such like. 'Mothers Of The Disappeared' was one such dark example of the new art that U2 typified. After Band Aid, rock too was maturing and confronting reality.

The song of the month for April 1987

Let It Be by Ferry Aid (peak chart position: No.1)

The tragedy of the Herald Of Free Enterprise capsizing at the port of Zeebrugge in early March prompted the latest well-intentioned fundraising single for the victims. Paul McCartney's classic composition was updated, with the great man himself lending his vocal support. Other pop luminaries such as Kate Bush weighed in with their contribution, and voila we had another chart-topping chart smash, which sounded better than the original.

The song of the month for May 1987

I Wanna Dance With Somebody (Who Loves Me) by Whitney Houston (peak chart position: No.1)

Now that Diana Ross and Tina Turner were in the twilight of their illustrious careers, a new African-American female singing sensation stepped into the large void vacated by their gradual disappearance. Whitney Houston was the latest pop wonder who would be a constant presence in hit parades for the subsequent decade. Her biggest smash to date was 'I Wanna Dance With Somebody (Who Loves Me)'. Many more hit singles would follow.

The song of the month for June 1987

Star Trekkin' by The Firm (peak chart position: No.1)

The enduring popularity of the science fiction series 'Star Trek' would prompt the latest novelty pop release. The Firm clinched a Number One position in the British chart with a daft little ditty which many music-buyers clearly found a liking for. The Firm had previously visited the UK singles lists with a tribute to the artful dodger Arfur Daley of Minder. 'Star Trekkin' was their finest glory and a reminder of the zany taste of UK music lovers.

The song of the month for July 1987

Who's That Girl? by Madonna (peak chart position: No.1)

Madonna's relentless pursuit of global domination continued in earnest as 'Who's That Girl' quickly followed 'La Isla Bonita' to the summit of the BBC Top 40. Madonna had also branched out into a less successful acting career. In fact she was such a household name that perhaps every High Court judge had probably even heard of her. Popular singers come and go but the genuinely talented Madonna was here to stay, like it or not.

The song of the month for August 1987

I Just Can't Stop Loving You by Michael Jackson With Siedah Garrett (peak chart position: No.1)

Michael Jackson renewed his onslaught upon both album and singles charts with ten new mouthwatering items from his exciting new long player, entitled 'Bad'. Although 'The Way You Make Me Feel' would be my choice as the best of a very good bunch, the first track to be lifted from the LP was the love song 'I Just Can't Stop Loving You.' Siedah Garrett was drafted in for this duet, but not before the superstar opened with the autobiographical lines:"A lot of people misunderstand me/That's because they don't really know me at all." 'Bad' was a worthy successor to the giants, 'Off The Wall' and 'Thriller'. Michael sang of being 'bad', but 'mad' seemed more apt.

The song of the month for September 1987

Kings Cross by The Pet Shop Boys (not released as a single)

Pop duos were in fashion in the eighties, what with the success of Erasure, Soft Cell, and Yazoo to name but three, but the best of them all was actually the Pet Shop Boys who actually released an album called 'Actually' in September. This project boasted such heavyweights as a collaboration with the pop legend, Dusty Springfield, as well as the big hits 'Heart', 'It's A Sin', and 'Rent'. However, the closing track 'Kings Cross' is one of the great undiscovered treasures in popular music. This atmospheric number is one of the highlights of the 1980s.

The song of the month for October 1987

China In Your Hands by T'Pau (peak chart position: No.1)

Carole Decker and her crew enjoyed the distinction of providing the British hit parade with the six hundredth Number One single. 'China In Your Hands' was an excellent pop song which deservedly lingered at the summit for a full month. The track featured a fine vocal performance from Decker as well as an equally good cameo from the saxophone. T'Pau were not one-hit wonders, yet they failed to replicate this commendable triumph.

The song of the month for November 1987

Build by The Housemartins (peak chart position: No.15)

The likeable, self-deprecating Housemartins hailed from Humberside, a fact they reminded everyone of with their album title 'London o Hull 4'. Paul Heaton and the lads had enjoyed a highly satisfactory 1986, courtesy of the chart-topping 'Caravan Of Love' and the jolly 'Happy Hour'. They had less commercial success thereafter but they did construct the admirable 'Build' which made an incursion into the Top Twenty near the end of 1987.

The song of the month for December 1987

Fairytale Of New York by The Pogues, Featuring Kirsty MacColl
(peak chart position: No.2)

Shane MacGowan became one of the most recognisable faces on the British music scene, with enough tooth decay to keep several dentists occupied. This Anglo-Irish vocalist remained sober long enough to record one of the great Christmas songs in the history of popular music. Kirsty MacColl, daughter of English folk singer Ewan MacColl, played the role of MacGowan's disillusioned other half in this mini-epic. Shane sang of envisaging "a better time when all our dreams come true". Unfortunately, Kirsty died in a boating accident in 2000, aged 41.

THE TOP 10 BEST SELLING UK SINGLES OF 1987

1 Never Gonna Give You Up by Rick Astley

2 Nothing's Gonna Stop Us Now by Starship

3 I Wanna Dance With Somebody by Whitney Houston

4 You Win Again by Bee Gees

5 China In Your Hand by T'Pau

6 Respectable by Mel & Kim

7 Stand By Me by Ben E King

8 It's A Sin by Pet Shop Boys

9 Pump Up The Volume by MARRS

10 Star Trekkin' by The Firm

ALBUM OF THE YEAR FOR 1987
The Joshua Tree by U2 (released in March)

Side 1:

1. Where the Streets Have No Name; 5:38

2. I Still Haven't Found What I'm Looking For; 4:38

3. With or Without You; 4:56

4. Bullet the Blue Sky; 4:32

5. Running to Stand Still; 4:18

Side 2:

1. Red Hill Mining Town; 4:54

2. In God's Country; 2:57

3. Trip Through Your Wires; 3:33

4. One Tree Hill; 5:23

5. Exit; 4:13

6. Mothers of the Disappeared; 5:12

Did the 1980s produce a better album than this? Here U2 make the transition from promising rock group to superstars with a project which was a refreshing break from the alpha male, macho posturing nonsense that characterised most 'great' rock outfits. Instead of which Bono and the gang get all introspective and spiritual with 'I Still Haven't Found What I'm Looking For'. More than anything the album reveals the band's conscience as they draw attention to the plight of South America's 'Mothers of the Disappeared'. 'The Joshua Tree' is a product of U2's growing fascination with America, be it the music scene, the culture, or the politics. The Dubliners were both intrigued and horrified by their discovery of America, north and south. This is conveyed on this seminal record. The fabulous foursome proceeded to world domination in the two decades hereafter, though it is doubtful whether anything they created quite compared with 'The Joshua Tree'. This magnificent LP is best appreciated in the dark, with the lights turned off, and sits comfortably alongside any classic album from any era.

THE UK NUMBER ONE ALBUMS OF 1987

17 Jan: Kate Bush – The Whole Story;	2 weeks
31 Jan: Paul Simon – Graceland;	3 weeks
21 Feb: London Stage Cast – The Phantom Of The Opera;	3 weeks
14 Mar: Hot Chocolate – The Very Best Of Hot Chocolate;	1 week
21 Mar: U2 – The Joshua Tree;	2 weeks
04 Apr: Various artist comp. (Virgin/EMI) –	
Now That's What I Call Music 9;	5 weeks
09 May: Curiosity Killed The Cat – Keep Your Distance;	2 weeks
23 May: Swing Out Sister – It's Better To Travel;	2 weeks
06 Jun: Simple Minds – Live In The City Of Light;	1 week
13 Jun: Whitney Houston – Whitney;	6 weeks
25 Jul: Terence Trent D'Arby – Introducing The Hardline;	1 week
01 Aug: Various artist comp. (CBS/WEA) – Hits 6;	4 weeks
29 Aug: Def Leppard – Hysteria;	1 week
05 Sep: Various artist comp. (CBS/WEA) – Hits 6;	1 week
12 Sep: Michael Jackson – Bad;	5 weeks
17 Oct: Bruce Springsteen – Tunnel Of Love;	1 week
24 Oct: Sting – Nothing Like The Sun;	1 week
31 Oct: Fleetwood Mac – Tango In The Night;	2 weeks
14 Nov: George Michael – Faith;	1 week
21 Nov: T'Pau – Bridge Of Spies;	1 week
28 Nov: Rick Astley – Whenever You Need Somebody;	1 week
05 Dec: Various artist comp. (EMI/Virgin) –	
Now That's What I Call Music 10;	6 weeks

THE US NUMBER ONE ALBUMS OF 1987

03 Jan: Bruce Springsteen – Live/1975–85;   2 weeks

17 Jan: Bon Jovi – Slippery When Wet;   7 weeks

07 Mar: The Beastie Boys – Licensed To Ill;   7 weeks

25 Apr: U2 – The Joshua Tree;   9 weeks

27 Jun: Whitney Houston – Whitney;   11 weeks

12 Sep: Soundtrack – La Bamba;   2 weeks

26 Sep: Michael Jackson – Bad;   6 weeks

07 Nov: Bruce Springsteen – Tunnel Of Love;   1 week

14 Nov: Soundtrack – Dirty Dancing;   7 weeks

THE UK NUMBER ONE SINGLES
OF 1987

24 Jan: Steve 'Silk' Hurley – Jack Your Body;   2 weeks

07 Feb: Aretha Franklin & George Michael –

      I Knew You Were Waiting (For Me);   2 weeks

21 Feb: Ben E King – Stand By Me;   3 weeks

14 Mar: Boy George – Everything I Own;   2 weeks

28 Mar: Mel & Kim – Respectable;   1 week

04 Apr: Ferry Aid – Let It Be;   3 weeks

25 Apr: Madonna – La Isla Bonita;   2 weeks

09 May: Starship – Nothing's Gonna Stop Us Now;   4 weeks

06 Jun: Whitney Houston –

      I Wanna Dance With Somebody (Who Loves Me);   2 weeks

20 Jun: The Firm – Star Trekkin';   2 weeks

04 Jul: Pet Shop Boys – It's A Sin;   3 weeks

25 Jul: Madonna – Who's That Girl;   1 week

01 Aug: Los Lobos – La Bamba;   2 weeks

15 Aug: Michael Jackson – I Just Can't Stop Loving You;   2 weeks

29 Aug: Rick Astley – Never Gonna Give You Up;   5 weeks

03 Oct: M/A/R/R/S – Pump Up The Volume;   2 weeks

17 Oct: Bee Gees – You Win Again;   4 weeks

14 Nov: T'Pau – China In Your Hand;   5 weeks

19 Dec: The Pet Shop Boys – Always On My Mind;   4 weeks

THE US NUMBER ONE SINGLES
OF 1987

03 Jan: The Bangles – Walk Like An Egyptian;		2 weeks
17 Jan: Gregory Abbott – Shake You Down;		1 week
24 Jan: Billy Vera And The Beaters – At This Moment;		2 weeks
07 Feb: Madonna – Open Your Heart;		1 week
14 Feb: Bon Jovi – Livin' On A Prayer;		4 weeks
14 Mar: Huey Lewis & The News – Jacob's Ladder;		1 week
21 Mar: Club Nouveau – Lean On Me;		2 weeks
04 Apr: Starship – Nothing's Gonna Stop Us Now;		2 weeks
18 Apr: Aretha Franklin & George Michael –		
I Knew You Were Waiting (For Me);		2 weeks
02 May: Cutting Crew – (I Just) Died In Your Arms;		2 weeks
16 May: U2 – With Or Without You;		3 weeks
06 Jun: Kim Wilde – You Keep Me Hangin' On;		1 week
13 Jun: Atlantic Starr – Always;		1 week
20 Jun: Lisa Lisa And Cult Jam – Head To Toe;		1 week
27 Jun: Whitney Houston – I Wanna Dance With Somebody		
(Who Loves Me);		2 weeks
11 Jul: Heart – Alone;		3 weeks
01 Aug: Bob Seger – Shakedown;		1 week
08 Aug: U2 – I Still Haven't Found What I'm Looking For;		2 weeks
22 Aug: Madonna – Who's That Girl;		1 week
29 Aug: Los Lobos – La Bamba;		3 weeks
19 Sep: Michael Jackson With Siedah Garrett –		
I Just Can't Stop Loving You;		1 week
26 Sep: Whitney Houston – Didn't We Almost Have It All;		2 weeks
10 Oct: Whitesnake – Here I Go Again;		1 week
17 Oct: Lisa Lisa And Cult Jam – Lost In Emotion;		1 week
24 Oct: Michael Jackson – Bad;		2 weeks
7 Nov: Tiffany – I Think We're Alone Now;		2 weeks
21 Nov: Billy Idol – Mony Mony;		1 week
28 Nov: Bill Medley & Jennifer Warnes – (I've Had) The Time Of My Life;		1 week
05 Dec: Belinda Carlisle – Heaven Is A Place On Earth;		1 week
12 Dec: George Michael – Faith;		3 weeks

THE 'UNSUCCESSFUL' UK NUMBER TWO SINGLES OF 1987

07 Feb: Pepsi And Shirlie – Heartache;	2 weeks
28 Feb: Percy Sledge – When A Man Loves A Woman;	2 weeks
25 Apr: Judy Boucher – Can't Be With You Tonight;	4 weeks
23 May: Tom Jones – A Boy From Nowhere;	1 week
13 Jun: Johnny Logan – Hold Me Now;	1 week
11 Jul: Bruce Willis – Under The Boardwalk;	2 weeks
22 Aug: Spagna – Call Me;	1 week
29 Aug: Pet Shop Boys & Dusty Springfield – What Have I Done To Deserve This;	2 weeks
12 Sep: The Fat Boys And The Beach Boys – Wipeout;	1 week
10 Oct: Abigail Mead & Nigel Goulding – Full Metal Jacket;	2 weeks
24 Oct: Jan Hammer – Crockett's Theme;	1 week
31 Oct: George Michael – Faith;	2 weeks
14 Nov: George Harrison – Got My Mind Set On You;	4 weeks
12 Dec: Rick Astley – When I Fall In Love;	2 weeks
26 Dec: The Pogues, Featuring Kirsty MacColl – Fairytale Of New York;	2 weeks

THE 'UNSUCCESSFUL' US NUMBER TWO SINGLES OF 1987

10 Jan: Duran Duran – Notorious

17 Jan: Robbie Nevil – C'est La Vie

21 Feb: The Georgia Satellites – Keep Your Hands To Yourself

14 Mar: Linda Ronstadt And James Ingram – Somewhere Out There

21 Mar: Janet Jackson – Let's Wait A While

25 Apr: Crowded House – Don't Dream It's Over

02 May: Jody Watley – Looking For A New Love

08 Aug: George Michael – I Want Your Sex

17 Oct: Prince – U Got The Look

24 Oct: Madonna – Causing A Commotion

19 Dec: Whitesnake – Is This Love

NEWS HIGHLIGHTS OF 1987

January 12th: Prince Edward resigns from the Royal Marines.

January 20th: Terry Waite goes missing in Beirut, feared kidnapped.

January 30th: The flotation of British Airways shares begins.

February 4th: The United States wins back yachting's America's Cup.

February 4th: Liberace dies. AIDS is rumoured to be the cause.

February 18th: Garrett Fitzgerald is defeated in the Irish election.

March 6th: The Herald of Free Enterprise capsizes at Zeebrugge.

March 10th: Charles Haughey becomes Taoiseach for a third time.

March 29th: The 'iron lady', Mrs Thatcher, pays a visit to Moscow.

April 7th: The Herald of Free Enterprise is refloated.

April 8th: Syrian troops end the siege of the Beirut Chatila camp.

April 22nd: Jim Callaghan is admitted to the Order of the Garter.

May 8th: 8 terrorists die in an SAS ambush in Loughgall.

May 11th: Mrs Thatcher calls a general election for June.

May 26th: Ernest Saunders quits as a director of Guinness.

June 12th: The Conservatives win the British general election.

June 20th: New Zealand win rugby union's first World Cup.

June 30th: Rupert Murdoch buys the Today newspaper.

July 3rd: Klaus Barbie is found guilty of aiding Nazi war atrocities.

July 12th: Nigel Mansell wins the British Grand Prix.

July 26th: Irish cyclist Stephen Roche wins the Tour de France.

August 20th: Michael Ryan kills fourteen people in Hungerford.

August 27th: Robert Maclennan becomes leader of the SDP.

August 30th: Ben Johnson sets a 100 metres world record.

September 5th: Eight die in an M6 motorway pile-up.

September 7th: Ford reveals that it has bought Aston Martin.

September 13th: The British Jockey Club approves Sunday racing.

October 15th:England suffers its worst storm for many years.

October 19th: The London Stock Exchange suffers a 'crash'.

October 23rd: Lester Piggott is jailed for tax evasion.

November 8th: A bomb explodes in Enniskillen on Remembrance Day.

November 8th: Australia win the cricket World Cup for the first time.

November 19th: A fire breaks out at King's Cross tube station.

December 8th: Gorbachev and Reagan agree on an arms reduction.

December 9th: Mike Gatting has a big row with a Pakistan umpire.

December 25th: Israelis launch a crackdown on Arab protesters.

SPORT IN 1987

English Division One football champions: Everton; runners-up: Liverpool

English FA Cup final: Coventry City 3 Tottenham Hotspur 2 (after extra time)

English League Cup Final: Arsenal 2 Liverpool 1

Scottish Premier League football champions: Glasgow Rangers; runners-up: Glasgow Celtic

Scottish FA Cup final: St. Mirren 1 Dundee United 0 (after extra time)

Scottish League Cup final: Glasgow Rangers 2 Glasgow Celtic 1

Irish League football champions: Linfield; Irish Cup final: Glentoran 1 Larne 0

League Of Ireland football champions: Shamrock Rovers; cup winners: Shamrock Rovers

European Cup final: FC Porto 2 Bayern Munich 1

European Cup-Winners' Cup final: Ajax 1 Lokomotive Leipzig 0

UEFA Cup final: IFK Goteborg beat Dundee United 2–1 on aggregate

English county cricket champions: Nottinghamshire

Five Nations' rugby union champions: France (the 'grand slam')

Formula One world drivers' champion: Nelson Piquet (Brazil) in a Williams car

Gaelic football All-Ireland champions: Meath; runners-up: Cork

British Open golf champion: Nick Faldo (at Muirfield)

US Masters golf champion: Larry Mize

US Open golf champion: Scott Simpson

USPGA golf champion: Larry Nelson

Rugby league Challenge Cup final: Halifax 19 St Helens 18

Wimbledon men's singles tennis final: P Cash beat I Lendl 7–6, 6–2, 7–5

Wimbledon ladies' singles tennis final: M Navratilova beat S Graf 7–5, 6–3

World snooker final: Steve Davis (England) beat Joe Johnson (England) 18–14

The Aintree Grand National steeplechase winner: Maori Venture; price 28–1

The Epsom Derby winner: Reference Point; jockey – Steve Cauthen; price 6–4F

The Ryder Cup: The United States Of America 13 Europe 15

1987's BUCKET-KICKERS

February 22nd: Andrew Warhola (US artist); aged 58

March 3rd: Danny Kaye (US actor); aged 74

April 17th: Carlton 'Carly' Barrett (Jamaican musician); aged 36

May 14th: Rita Hayworth (US actress); aged 68

June 3rd: Andres Segovia (Spanish guitarist); aged 94

June 22nd: Fred Astaire (US dancer); aged 88

August 17th: Rudolf Hess (ex-German politician); aged 93

August 28th: John Huston (US director); aged 81

August 29th: Lee Marvin (US actor); aged 63

September 11th: Peter Tosh (Jamaican musician); aged 42

September 16th: Arthur Christopher John Soames (British politician); aged 66

October 19th: Jacqueline du Pre (British cellist); aged 42

November 5th: Eamonn Andrews (Irish broadcaster); aged 64

December 10th: Jascha Heifetz (US violinist); aged 86

The song of the month for January 1988

Gimme Hope Jo'anna by Eddy Grant (peak chart position: No.7)

Veteran Caribbean performer Eddy Grant had put in appearances in the British hit parade in the two previous decades with the likes of the poptastic 'Baby Come Back' with the Equals in 1968 and then the formidable 'Living On The Frontline' in 1979. Guyana's greatest singer stepped out of Electric Avenue to address the running sore of apartheid. Far from appealing to a lover called Joanna, Grant was urging Johannesburg to come to her senses and embrace democracy. The worthy sentiments were eventually heeded a few years later.

The song of the month for February 1988

I'm Not Scared by Eighth Wonder (peak chart position: No.7)

1988 was a year that witnessed much chart action from the fairer sex as the likes of Belinda Carlisle, Jane Wiedlin, Tiffany, and Kylie Minogue all invaded the airwaves. However, there was a new trend for groups fronted by an eye-catching female, as pioneered by Blondie and the Pretenders. Transvision Vamp and Voice Of The Beehive were two such bands along with the short-lived Eighth Wonder. The latter featured the blonde bombshell Patsy Kensit. Patsy and her male companions released the fine pop song, 'I'm Not Scared'. They had previously contributed the excellent 'Having It All' for the 'Absolute Beginners' soundtrack.

The song of the month for March 1988

I Pronounce You by The Madness (peak chart position: No.44)

Camden Town's finest act had called it a day, and effectively split in two. The likeable Suggs and co-vocalist Carl Smyth decided to remain slightly mad and they consequently released an album which flopped, but which contained a number of quirky delights, such as the minor hit 'I Pronounce You'. This unusual wedding song included the sound of a sitar from the semi-mad guitarist Chris Foreman. It's worth checking out, if you're mad.

The song of the month for April 1988

There Is Always Something There To Remind Me by The Housemartins
(peak chart position: No.35)

Shortly before the Housemartins flew the nest and reinvented themselves in the Beautiful South and in the guise of Fatboy Slim, they signed off with the delightful 'There Is Always Something There To Remind Me' which should not be confused with Sandie Shaw's superb Number One from 1964. Hull's greatest foursome released a 'quite good' compilation which amusingly detailed the impact of their songs upon the likes of New Zealand.

The song of the month for May 1988

With A Little Help From My Friends by Wet Wet Wet
(peak chart position: No.1)

After the monumental triumph of Band Aid, there seemed no end to pop acts who wished to volunteer for a charity single. Now it was the turn of Scotland's Wet Wet Wet who shrewdly dipped into the Beatles' catalogue, thus ensuring a smash hit. This was the second time that this Sergeant Pepper track had been successfully covered. To be fair, both Joe Cocker's version and this pop interpretation were improvements on the original. Meanwhile, Billy Bragg was on the flip side,with his attempt at the Fab Four's 'She's Leaving Home'.

The song of the month for June 1988

Breakfast In Bed by UB40 With Chrissie Hynde (peak chart position: No.6)

Whilst Wet Wet Wet delighted many with their breezy cover version, UB40 and their old mate Chrissie Hynde re-united for a bash at an old reggae hit. This updated interpretation of 'Breakfast In Bed' was infinitely superior to 'I Got You Babe' though less successful. Encouraged by this new success, UB40 couldn't resist the temptation to return to the studio a year later and release another 'Labour Of Love' album entirely of covers.

The song of the month for July 1988

The Only Way Is Up by Yazz And The Plastic Population
(peak chart position: No.1)

The summer sensation of 1988 was 'The Only Way Is Up' which was a regular ingre-
dient in all disco nights out as even I can testify. Far from being merely an energetic toe-tapper, this brilliant dancefloor favourite actually possessed uplifting lyrics
and was less 'empty' than many dance songs. It was a pity however that Yazz then
descended into the banality of 'Stand Up For Your Love Rights'. 'The Only Way' was
the year's 2nd biggest seller.

The song of the month for August 1988

Teardrops by Womack And Womack (peak chart position: No.3)

The universally respected musical duo of Womack and Womack enjoyed much
deserved success with the ascent of 'Teardrops' towards the peak of the BBC Top Forty.
This marvellous single was unquestionably one of the best pop songs to emerge from
an American recording studio in the 'eighties. 'Teardrops' featured in the duo's fourth
long player, entitled 'Conscience', and it did manage to achieve chart-topping glory in
the Netherlands.

The song of the month for September 1988

Storms In Africa by Enya (peak chart position: No.41)

The magnificent Enya enchanted music aficionados with a brand new album of sounds
that were markedly different from anything else on the airwaves. The towering track
of the 'Watermark' project is arguably 'Storms In Africa'. Enya brews up a musical
storm here with a quality recording decorated by a combination of a formidable drum-
beat and sumptuous vocals. Never has a storm seemed more attractive. This monster
of a single failed to impress the UK's music lovers, but then they did prefer Bros, Kylie
and Jason. Enough said.

The song of the month for October 1988

Elephant Stone by The Stone Roses (peak chart position: No.8 in 1990)

The pop pendulum had swung from the Mersey sound to the mods and then punks of London and then back oop north to Lancashire where Manchester would become the new mecca for British youth. The latest big thing were the Stone Roses. It took this four man combo a few attempts to find their feet, but in October 1988 they released 'Elephant Stone' with its elephant riff and awesome drums. The world of music had changed for good.

The song of the month for November 1988

In Your Room by The Bangles (peak chart position: No.35)

Long before the Spice Girls took the world by storm, the Bangles spiced up our lives with a series of terrific singles. 'Manic Monday' and 'Walk Like An Egyptian' were monster smashes from the fine 'A Different Light' album. Its successor, 'Everything' is less appealing, though it contains the superb 'Be With You' and 'Eternal Flame'. However, its best item is perhaps the seductive 'In Your Room'. Susanna Hoffs sounds and looks even more irresistible than ever. Why oh why didn't British record buyers recognise the quality of this ace pop tune?

The song of the month for December 1988

Fine Time by New Order (peak chart position: No.11)

The enigmatic New Order were indeed enjoying a fine time as the 1980s unfolded. Tracks such as 'Thieves Like Us', 'The Perfect Kiss' and 'Bizarre Love Triangle' were giants on the music landscape. The foursome then tapped into the techno-rhythms of the emerging Ibiza dance scene to construct the 'Technique' album. This new LP opens with the infectious 'Fine Time'. If there was any justice, it should have stayed at No.1 for months.

THE TOP 10 BEST SELLING UK SINGLES OF 1988

1 Mistletoe And Wine by Cliff Richard

2 The Only Way Is Up by Yazz & The Plastic Population

3 I Should Be So Lucky by Kylie Minogue

4 Especially For You by Kylie Minogue & Jason Donovan

5 I Think We're Alone Now by Tiffany

6 Nothing's Gonna Change My Love For You by Glenn Medeiros

7 A Groovy Kind Of Love by Phil Collins

8 With A Little Help From My Friends by Wet Wet Wet

9 He Ain't Heavy He's My Brother by The Hollies

10 Teardrops by Womack & Womack

ALBUM OF THE YEAR FOR 1988

Watermark by Enya (released in September)

Side 1:

1. Watermark; 2:24

2. Cursum Perficio; 4:06

3. On Your Shore; 3:59

4. Storms In Africa; 4:03

5. Exile; 4:20

6. Miss Clare Remembers; 1:59

Side 2:

1. Orinoco Flow; 4:25

2. Evening Falls; 3:46

3. River; 3:10

4. The Longships; 3:36

5. Na Laetha Geal M'Oige; 3:54

By the late 'eighties celtic music was very much in vogue, whether it be the Pogues, Hothouse Flowers, the Waterboys, Scotland's Proclaimers, or even U2. However, the latest sensation from the Emerald Isle, Enya, stepped forth with sounds that simply took the breath away. The 'Watermark' album is frequently categorised as 'easy listening' which is an apt description, but it was of sufficient commercial appeal to attract record buyers of all ages. The instruments are almost exclusively performed by Enya who also composes all the music, with the lyrical assistance of Roma Ryan. The long player possesses three wonderful instrumentals, namely 'The Longships', the beauty of the piano-dominated title track, and the item entitled 'River' which is decorated by excellent keyboards. Enya's decision to fly away from the Brennan family nest had clearly paid dividends, especially when 'Orinoco Flow' sailed away to the Number One position in the British charts. 'Cursum Perficio' is also worthy of mention as the title is drawn from the inscription over Marilyn Monroe's house, meaning 'my journey ends here'. Enya continued to delight music aficionados with further similar records. When you can conjure such magical music, why wander away from a winning formula?

THE UK NUMBER ONE ALBUMS OF 1988

16 Jan: Wet Wet Wet – Popped In Souled Out;	1 week
23 Jan: Johnny Hates Jazz – Turn Back The Clock;	1 week
30 Jan: Terence Trent D'Arby – Introducing The Hardline;	8 weeks
26 Mar: Morrissey – Viva Hate;	1 week
02 Apr: Various artist comp. (EMI/Virgin) –	
Now That's What I Call Music 11;	3 weeks
23 Apr: Iron Maiden – Seventh Son Of A Seventh Son;	1 week
30 Apr: Erasure – The Innocents;	1 week
07 May: Fleetwood Mac – Tango In The Night;	2 weeks
21 May: Prince – Lovesexy;	1 week
28 May: Fleetwood Mac – Tango In The Night;	1 week
04 Jun: Various artist comp. (CBS) – Nite Flite;	4 weeks
02 Jul: Tracy Chapman – Tracy Chapman;	3 weeks
23 Jul: Various artist comp. (EMI/Virgin) –	
Now That's What I Call Music 12;	5 weeks
27 Aug: Kylie Minogue – Kylie – The Album;	4 weeks
24 Sep: Various artist comp. (Vertigo) – Hot City Nights;	1 week
01 Oct: Bon Jovi – New Jersey;	2 weeks
15 Oct: Chris de Burgh – Flying Colours;	1 week
22 Oct: U2 – Rattle And Hum;	1 week
29 Oct: Dire Straits – Money For Nothing;	3 weeks
19 Nov: Kylie Minogue – Kylie – The Album;	2 weeks
03 Dec: Various artist comp. (EMI/Virgin) –	
Now That's What I Call Music 13;	3 weeks
24 Dec: Cliff Richard – Private Collection 1979–1988;	2 weeks

THE US NUMBER ONE ALBUMS OF 1988

02 Jan: Soundtrack – Dirty Dancing;	2 weeks
16 Jan: George Michael – Faith;	1 week
23 Jan: Tiffany – Tiffany;	2 weeks
06 Feb: George Michael – Faith;	5 weeks
12 Mar: Soundtrack – Dirty Dancing;	9 weeks
14 May: George Michael – Faith;	6 weeks
25 Jun: Van Halen – OU812;	4 weeks
23 Jul: Def Leppard – Hysteria;	2 weeks
06 Aug: Guns N' Roses – Appetite For Destruction;	1 week
13 Aug: Def Leppard – Hysteria;	1 week
20 Aug: Steve Winwood – Roll With It;	1 week
27 Aug: Tracy Chapman – Tracy Chapman;	1 week
03 Sep: Def Leppard – Hysteria;	3 weeks
24 Sep; Guns N' Roses – Appetite For Destruction;	3 weeks
15 Oct: Bon Jovi – October;	4 weeks
12 Nov: U2 – Rattle And Hum;	6 weeks
24 Dec: Anita Baker – Giving You The Best That I Got;	2 weeks

THE UK NUMBER ONE SINGLES
OF 1988

16 Jan: Belinda Carlisle – Heaven Is A Place On Earth;	2 weeks
30 Jan: Tiffany – I Think We're Alone Now;	3 weeks
20 Feb: Kylie Minogue – I Should Be So Lucky;	5 weeks
26 Mar: Aswad – Don't Turn Around;	2 weeks
09 Apr: The Pet Shop Boys – Heart;	3 weeks
30 Apr: S'Express – Theme from S'Express;	2 weeks
14 May: Fairground Attraction – Perfect;	1 week
21 May: Wet Wet Wet – With A Little Help From My Friends;	4 weeks
18 Jun: The Timelords – Doctorin' The Tardis;	1 week
25 Jun: Bros – I Owe You Nothing;	2 weeks
09 Jul: Glenn Medeiros – Nothing's Gonna Change My Love For You;	4 weeks
06 Aug: Yazz & The Plastic Population – The Only Way Is Up;	5 weeks
10 Sep: Phil Collins – A Groovy Kind Of Love;	2 weeks
24 Sep: The Hollies – He Ain't Heavy He's My Brother;	2 weeks
08 Oct: U2 – Desire;	1 week
15 Oct: Whitney Houston – One Moment In Time;	2 weeks
29 Oct: Enya – Orinoco Flow (Sail Away);	3 weeks
19 Nov: Robin Beck – The First Time;	3 weeks
10 Dec: Cliff Richard – Mistletoe & Wine;	4 weeks

THE US NUMBER ONE SINGLES OF 1988

02 Jan: George Michael – Faith;	1 week
09 Jan: Whitney Houston – So Emotional;	1 week
16 Jan: George Harrison – Got My Mind Set On You;	1 week
23 Jan: Michael Jackson – The Way You Make Me Feel;	1 week
30 Jan: INXS – Need You Tonight;	1 week
06 Feb: Tiffany – Could've Been;	2 weeks
20 Feb: Expose – Seasons Change;	1 week
27 Feb: George Michael – Father Figure;	2 weeks
12 Mar: Rick Astley – Never Gonna Give You Up;	2 weeks
26 Mar: Michael Jackson – Man In The Mirror;	2 weeks
09 Apr: Billy Ocean – Get Outta My Dreams, Get Into My Car;	2 weeks
23 Apr: Whitney Houston – Where Do Broken Hearts Go;	2 weeks
07 May: Terence Trent D'Arby – Wishing Well;	1 week
14 May: Gloria Estefan & Miami Sound Machine – Anything For You;	2 weeks
28 May: George Michael – One More Try;	3 weeks
18 Jun: Rick Astley – Together Forever;	1 week
25 Jun: Debbie Gibson – Foolish Beat;	1 week
02 Jul: Michael Jackson – Dirty Diana;	1 week
09 Jul: Cheap Trick – The Flame;	2 weeks
23 Jul: Richard Marx – Hold On To The Nights;	1 week
30 Jul: Steve Winwood – Roll With It;	4 weeks
27 Aug: George Michael – Monkey;	2 weeks
10 Sep: Guns N' Roses – Sweet Child O' Mine;	2 weeks
24 Sep: Bobby McFerrin – Don't Worry, Be Happy;	2 weeks
08 Oct: Def Leppard – Love Bites;	1 week
15 Oct: UB40 – Red Red Wine;	1 week
22 Oct: Phil Collins – Groovy Kind Of Love;	2 weeks
05 Nov: The Beach Boys – Kokomo;	1 week
12 Nov: Wild, Wild West – The Escape Club;	1 week
19 Nov: Bon Jovi – Bad Medicine;	2 weeks
03 Dec: Will To Power – Baby, I Love Your Way/Freebird Medley;	1 week
10 Dec: Chicago – Look Away;	2 weeks
24 Dec: Poison – Every Rose Has Its Thorn;	2 weeks

THE 'UNSUCCESSFUL' UK NUMBER TWO HIT SINGLES OF 1988

23 Jan: Terence Trent D'Arby – Sign Your Name;	1 week
06 Feb: Bros – When Will I Be Famous;	1 week
27 Feb: Bomb The Bass – Beat Dis;	2 weeks
12 Mar: Rick Astley – Together Forever;	2 weeks
26 Mar: Bros – Drop The Boy;	4 weeks
23 Apr: Climie Fisher – Love Changes Everything;	1 week
28 May: Kylie Minogue – Got To Be Certain;	3 weeks
02 Jul: The Fat Boys With Chubby Checker – The Twist (Yo, Twist!);	2 weeks
16 Jul: Salt N Pepa – Push It/Tramp;	3 weeks
06 Aug: Kylie Minogue – The Loco-Motion;	4 weeks
03 Sep: Brother Beyond – The Harder I Try;	2 weeks
22 Oct: Bobby McFerrin – Don't Worry, Be Happy;	1 week
29 Oct: Kylie Minogue – Je Ne Sais Pas Pourquoi;	3 weeks
19 Nov: Yazz – Stand Up For Your Love Rights;	1 week
26 Nov: INXS – Need You Tonight;	1 week
03 Dec: Bros – Cat Among The Pigeons / Silent Night;	1 week

THE 'UNSUCCESSFUL' US NUMBER TWO HIT SINGLES OF 1988:

30 Jan: The Bangles – Hazy Shade Of Winter

13 Feb: Pet Shop Boys & Dusty Springfield – What Have I Done To Deserve This

19 Mar: Belinda Carlisle – I Get Weak

26 Mar: Richard Marx – Endless Summer Nights

16 Apr: INXS – Devil Inside

14 May: Johnny Hates Jazz – Shattered Dreams

09 Jul: Pebbles – Mercedes Boy

23 Jul: Def Leppard – Pour Some Sugar On Me

06 Aug: Breathe – Hands To Heaven

27 Aug: Elton John – I Don't Want To Go On With You Like That

10 Sep: Robert Palmer – Simply Irresistible

NEWS HIGHLIGHTS OF 1988

January 10th: Willie Whitelaw resigns as Leader of the House of Commons.
January 17th: President Ortega offers a cease-fire in Nicaragua.
January 25th: A radical review of the National Health Service is announced.
February 5th: Red nose day is held in Britain for Comic Relief.
February 9th: The House of Commons agrees to be televised in future.
February 29th: Archbishop Tutu is arrested in South Africa.
March 7th: Three Irish terrorists are killed in Gibraltar.
March 10th: Prince Charles narrowly escapes death in an Alpine avalanche.
March 19th: Two British soldiers are lynched at a west Belfast funeral.
April 3rd: India seals the border between the Punjab and Pakistan.
April 5th: A Kuwaiti airliner is hijacked in Iran.
April 20th: Hostages are freed from the Kuwaiti Airlines Jumbo.
May 10th: Francois Mitterand is re-elected President of France.
May 18th: Sikh militants end their siege of Amritsar's Golden Temple.
May 31st: Ronald Reagan performs a charm offensive in Moscow.
June 2nd: Interest rates in Britain are increased to eight per cent.
June 9th: Mike Gatting is sacked as England cricket captain.
June 11th: A Wembley concert celebrates Nelson Mandela's 70th birthday.
July 6th: The Piper Alpha oil rig suffers an explosion and fire.
July 16th: Michael Jackson starts his British tour at Wembley.
July 24th: Spanish cyclist Pedro Delgado wins the Tour de France.
August 8th: England lose yet another test match to the West Indies.
August 8th: Iran and Iraq agree a cease-fire to their war.
August 11th: Sudan is on the receiving end of a massive flood.
September 2nd: Isabel Allende returns to Chile from exile.
September 10th: Steffi Graf completes the tennis 'Grand Slam'.
September 24th: Ben Johnson 'wins' the Olympic Games 100 metres.
October 6th: General Pinochet loses in Chile's general election.
October 16th: Ireland win golf's Dunhill Cup at St.Andrew's.
October 28th: A riot occurs at Wenceslas Square in Prague.
November 2nd: Yitzhak Shamir's Likud Party wins Israel's general election.
November 8th: George Bush is elected President of the United States.
November 11th: Mrs Thatcher meets Lech Walesa at the Gdansk shipyard.
December 7th: An earthquake in Armenia claims 100,000 lives.
December 12th: 36 die in a rail disaster at Clapham Junction.
December 22nd: An American jet explodes and crashes onto Lockerbie

SPORT IN 1988

English Division One football champions: Liverpool; runners-up: Manchester United

English FA Cup final: Wimbledon 1 Liverpool 0

English League Cup Final: Luton Town 3 Arsenal 2

Scottish Premier League football champions: Glasgow Celtic; runners-up: Heart Of Midlothian

Scottish FA Cup final: Glasgow Celtic 2 Dundee United 1

Scottish League Cup final: Glasgow Rangers beat Aberdeen 5–3 on penalties

Irish League football champions: Glentoran; Irish Cup final: Glentoran 1 Glenavon 0

League Of Ireland football champions: Dundalk; cup winners: Dundalk

European Cup final: PSV Eindhoven beat Benfica on penalties; 0–0 after extra time

European Cup-Winners' Cup final: KV Mechelen 1 Ajax 0

UEFA Cup final: Bayer Leverkusen beat Espanyol 3–2 on penalties; 3–3 on aggregate

English county cricket champions: Worcestershire

Five Nations' rugby union champions: France and Wales (both 6 points); Wales (the 'triple crown')

Formula One world drivers' champion: Ayrton Senna (Brazil) in a McLaren car

Gaelic football All-Ireland champions: Meath; runners-up: Cork

British Open golf champion: Seve Ballesteros (at Royal Lytham & St. Annes)

US Masters golf champion: Sandy Lyle

US Open golf champion: Curtis Strange

USPGA golf champion: Jeff Sluman

Rugby league Challenge Cup final: Wigan 32 Halifax 12

Wimbledon men's singles tennis final: S Edberg beat B Becker 4–6, 7–6, 6–4, 6–2

Wimbledon ladies' singles tennis final: S Graf beat M Navratilova 5–7, 6–2, 6–1

World snooker final: Steve Davis (England) beat Terry Griffiths (Wales) 18–11

The Aintree Grand National steeplechase winner: Rhyme 'N' Reason; price 10–1

The Epsom Derby winner: Kahyasi; jockey – Ray Cochrane; price 11–1

European Championship final: Netherlands 2 USSR 0 (in Munich)

1988's BUCKET-KICKERS

January 7th: Trevor Wallace Howard (British actor); aged 71

January 15th: Sean McBride (ex-Irish politician); aged 83

January 28th: Dr Emil Julius Klaus Fuchs (ex-German spy); aged 76

February 14th: Fritz Loewe (US composer); aged 86

February 15th: Richard Phillips Feynman (US physicist); aged 69

April 14th: John Stonehouse (ex-British politician); aged 62

April 15th: Kenneth Williams (British actor); aged 62

April 23rd; Lord Ramsey (British clergyman); aged 83

April 28th: Fenner Brockway (British politician); aged 99

May 11th: H.A.R. 'Kim' Philby (ex-British spy); aged 76

June 8th: Russell Harty (British broadcaster); aged 53

July 20th: Charles Mark Edward Boxer (British cartoonist); aged 57

August 14th: Enzo Ferrari (Italian businessman); aged 90

August 17th: Zia ul-Haq (Pakistan's President); aged 64

August 19th: Sir Frederick Ashton (British choreographer); aged 83

September 12th: Roger Hargreaves (British illustrator); aged 70

October 2nd: Sir Alexander Arnold Constantine Issigonis (British inventor); aged 81

October 9th: John Edward Thompson 'Jackie' Milburn (British footballer); aged 64

November 19th: Christina Onassis (Greek tycoon); aged 37

December 6th: Roy Orbison (US singer); aged 52

The song of the month for January 1989

Fisherman's Blues by The Waterboys (peak chart position: No.32)

'Fisherman's Blues' was undeniably one of the great albums of the decade, helped by the introductory track of the same name. Here is one of those numbers that one would find impossible to sit still to. Mike Scott yearns to be a fisherman out on the sea "far away from dry land and its bitter memories." I can dig that, brother. The words include such imagery as "crashing headlong into the heartland like a cannon in the rain". What a song.

The song of the month for February 1989

Nothing Has Been Proved by Dusty Springfield (peak chart position: No.16)

'Sixties singing sensation Dusty Springfield experienced a new burst of life after having been championed and encouraged by the Pet Shop Boys. Chris and Neil were on hand to provide musical assistance to this majestic single which had its origins in the closing credits of the superb film, 'Scandal'. Previously, 'What Have I Done To Deserve This' narrowly failed to hit No.1 and now the lukewarm response to this new item was another scandal.

The song of the month for March 1989

Oh Father by Madonna (peak chart position: No.16 in 1996)

Madonna, as only she could, succeeded in delighting one half of the population and enraging the other half with her new album 'Like A Prayer'. Folks were confused by what they perceived as moralising one moment and seduction and sexuality the next. Whatever the truth, the new album contained the dark 'Oh Father'. Here the singer recounts an abusive upbringing which many of her young fans could possibly relate to. Such are the slings and arrows of outrageous fortune, but this epic item is far superior to many of her biggest sellers.

The song of the month for April 1989

If You Don't Know Me By Now by Simply Red (peak chart position: No.2)

It wasn't until the autumn of 1995 that Mick and his partners would travel to the top of the hit parade on their fairground rollercoaster ride. Back in the 'eighties, Simply Red were responsible for two of the most popular songs of the decade. 'Holding Back The Years' was one of the best singles of 1986, and three years later the group were giving their own creditable soul assessment of this old hit by Harold Melvin And The Blue Notes.

The song of the month for May 1989

Disappointed by Public Image Limited (peak chart position: No.38)

John Lydon had gradually retreated from the public domain after the notoriety of his existence as the infamous Johnny Rotten. Lydon continued to record with Public Image Limited at various intervals. They failed to put compilers of the charts to any trouble terribly often, but they still came forth with the occasional gold nugget. In 'Disappointed' Lydon scoffs about how "friendship rears its ugly head." The guy was a true individual'.

The song of the month for June 1989

Negative Creep by Nirvana (not released as a single)

Would-be rock stars Nirvana took their first steps on a phenomenal path to fame with the release of their debut album, 'Bleach'. Still very much a cult act from Seattle, the self-confessed former nerd Kurt Cobain was already revealing his grunge power chords and songs of self-loathing and insecurity. 'Negative Creep' spoke to a lot of the disillusioned young people of Generation X who felt alienated by the so-called 'American dream.'

The song of the month for July 1989

Misty Morning Albert Bridge by The Pogues (peak chart position: No.41)

The Pogues may have previously performed items related to the 'majestic Shannon' and to Kilkenny, but they were equally sentimental about London, hence the tracks 'White City' and this outstanding composition. Sexy Shane 'sings' from the viewpoint of a soul incarcerated abroad in a jail or even hotel room who dreams of a reunion with his sweetheart on a misty morning at the west end's Albert Bridge. The accompanying music is of the highest quality. This is yet another reminder that 'eighties music had songs that other eras could only envy.

The song of the month for August 1989

Stand by R.E.M. (peak chart position: No.48)

Georgia's R.E.M. had spent several years cultivating a following. Now they were reaching new audiences with the success of their recent album, called 'Green'. One of the long player's products was 'Stand' and this fine rocker would succeed in standing in the British singles list in the late summer of 1989. It might have stood a lot higher but regrettably Jive Bunny was the flavour of the month. R.E.M. however were on the brink of glory.

The song of the month for September 1989

Sowing The Seeds Of Love by Tears For Fears (peak chart position: No.5)

It was like Sergeant Pepper all over again when Tears For Fears delivered their very own peace and love anthem. There may no longer have been enough hippies or flower power devotees around to dig the sentiments of this single, but it had sufficient class to reach out to many music enthusiasts. Curt and Roland had contributed enormously to the rich tapestry of the 1980s. This Top 5 hit was arguably their greatest legacy.

The song of the month for October 1989

All Around The World by Lisa Stansfield (peak chart position: No.1)

Rochdale's finest female vocalist had the difficult task of competing in the market-place against the plethora of Stock, Aitken And Waterman creations which appeared to monopolise the singles listings, but she managed to succeed with an absolute peach of a pop song. The subject matter of the tune may have been far from happy, but Lisa's desire to find her man and make amends certainly struck a chord with Britain's fickle record buyers.

The song of the month for November 1989

Fools Gold by The Stone Roses (peak chart position: No.8)

As the eighties drew to a close, the new decade beckoned with endless opportunities for Manchester's Fab Four. They had now unleashed a remarkable double A-side featuring 'Fools Gold' which belonged in both the disc collections of indie followers and dance disciples. This song sounded so cool and sexy that it looked like game, set and match to its authors, courtesy of Ian Brown's hushed vocals and John Squire's wah-wah guitar. The other side was 'What The World Is Waiting For'. Over the course of the next few years the world waited for more material, but the enigmatic Roses vanished into a labyrinth of record company disputes and also drugs.

The song of the month for December 1989

Brite Side by Deborah Harry (peak chart position: No.59)

The 1980s began with the triumph of 'Atomic' in the British chart, and although Blondie accumulated two more chart-toppers before the end of that year, Debbie Harry then experienced fluctuating fortunes in the rest of the decade. The hits may have dried up but Deborah refused to capitulate. The hit parade may be a playground for the young but Debs was still present in the charts at the end of the 'eighties with the aptly-titled 'Brite Side'.

THE TOP 10 BEST SELLING UK SINGLES OF 1989

1 Ride On Time by Black Box

2 Swing The Mood by Jive Bunny & The Mastermixers

3 Eternal Flame by The Bangles

4 Too Many Broken Hearts by Jason Donovan

5 Back To Life by Soul II Soul

6 Something's Gotten Hold Of My Heart by Marc Almond & Gene Pitney

7 That's What I Like by Jive Bunny & The Mastermixers

8 Pump Up The Jam by Technotronic

9 Do They Know It's Christmas by Band Aid II

10 Like A Prayer by Madonna

ALBUM OF THE YEAR FOR 1989:
The Stone Roses by The Stone Roses (released in March)

Side 1:

1. I Wanna Be Adored; 4:52

2. She Bangs the Drums; 3:42

3. Waterfall; 4:37

4. Don't Stop; 5:17

5. Bye Bye Badman; 4:00

Side 2:

1. Elizabeth My Dear; 0:59

2. (Song for My) Sugar Spun Sister; 3:25

3. Made of Stone; 4:10

4. Shoot You Down; 4:10

5. This Is the One; 4:58

6. I Am the Resurrection; 8:12

After punk had petered out a decade earlier followed by the rapid rise and then demise of Two Tone, British working-class youth failed to provide a new movement that would revolutionise planet pop until the emergence of the 'Madchester' indie scene at the end of the 'eighties. Spearheading this new craze were such crazies as the Happy Mondays and the Stone Roses. Whilst the footballing giants of Manchester continued to under-perform, here were Mancunian acts determined to leave their mark on the music world. It was the four 'Roses' who spearheaded the latest musical trend with a project which has been hailed as unquestionably the masterpiece of its era. Here was a group with so much confidence, it could have been mistaken for arrogance. However when you just happen to possess one of the world's best young guitarists in John Squire, not to mention the impressive drumming from Mani, well how can you possibly fail? The outro for example on 'Waterfall' is simply stunning, whilst the prolonged psychedelic jam at the end of 'I Am The Resurrection' far surpasses anything from the much-trumpeted late 'sixties. This album is a giant. 'Britpop' started back here.

THE UK NUMBER ONE ALBUMS
OF 1989

07 Jan: Various artist comp. (EMI/Virgin) – Now That's What I Call Music 13;	1 week
14 Jan: Erasure – The Innocents;	1 week
21 Jan: Roy Orbison – The Legendary Roy Orbison;	3 weeks
11 Feb: New Order – Technique;	1 week
18 Feb: Fine Young Cannibals – The Raw And The Cooked;	1 week
25 Feb: Simply Red – A New Flame;	4 weeks
25 Mar: Gloria Estefan & Miami Sound Machine – Anything For You;	1 week
01 Apr: Madonna – Like A Prayer;	2 weeks
15 Apr: Deacon Blue – When The World Knows Your Name;	2 weeks
29 Apr: Simply Red – A New Flame;	1 week
06 May: Holly Johnson – Blast!;	1 week
13 May: Simple Minds – Street Fighting Years;	1 week
20 May: Jason Donovan – Ten Good Reasons;	2 weeks
03 Jun: Queen – The Miracle;	1 week
10 Jun: Jason Donovan – Ten Good Reasons;	2 weeks
24 Jun: Paul McCartney – Flowers In The Dirt;	1 week
01 Jul: Prince – Batman (OST);	1 week
08 Jul: Transvision Vamp – Velveteen;	1 week
15 Jul: Soul II Soul – Club Classics Volume One;	1 week
22 Jul: Simply Red: A New Flame;	2 weeks
05 Aug: Gloria Estefan – Cuts Both Ways;	6 weeks
16 Sep: London Stage Cast – Aspects Of Love;	1 week
23 Sep: Eurythmics – We Too Are One;	1 week
30 Sep: Tina Turner – Foreign Affair;	1 week
07 Oct: Tears For Fears – The Seeds Of Love;	1 week
14 Oct: Tracy Chapman – Crossroads;	1 week
21 Oct: Kylie Minogue – Enjoy Yourself;	1 week
28 Oct: Erasure – Wild!;	2 weeks
11 Nov: Chris Rea – The Road To Hell;	3 weeks
02 Dec: Phil Collins – ... But Seriously;	5 weeks

THE US NUMBER ONE ALBUMS OF 1989

07 Jan: Anita Baker – Giving You The Best That I Got;	2 weeks
21 Jan: Bobby Brown – Don't Be Cruel;	3 weeks
11 Feb: Guns N' Roses – Appetite For Destruction;	1 week
18 Feb: Bobby Brown – Don't Be Cruel;	3 weeks
11 Mar: Debbie Gibson – Electric Youth;	5 weeks
15 Apr: Tone Loc – Loc–ed After Dark;	1 week
22 Apr: Madonna – Like A Prayer;	6 weeks
03 Jun: Fine Young Cannibals – The Raw And The Cooked;	7 weeks
22 Jul: Prince/Soundtrack – Batman;	6 weeks
02Sep: Richard Marx – Repeat Offender;	1 week
09 Sep: The New Kids On The Block – Hangin' Tough;	2 weeks
23 Sep: Milli Vanilli – Girl You Know It's True;	2 weeks
07 Oct: Paula Abdul – Forever Your Girl;	1 week
14 Oct: Motley Crue – Dr.Feelgood;	2 weeks
28 Oct: Janet Jackson – Rhythm Nation 1814;	4 weeks
25 Nov: Milli Vanilli – Girl You Know It's True;	3 weeks
16 Dec: Billy Joel – Storm Front;	1 week
23 Dec: Milli Vanilli – Girl You Know It's True;	1 week
30 Dec: Phil Collins – …But Seriously	

THE UK NUMBER ONE SINGLES
OF 1989

07 Jan: Kylie Minogue & Jason Donovan – Especially For You;	3 weeks
28 Jan: Marc Almond & Gene Pitney –	
Somethings Gotten Hold Of My Heart;	4 weeks
25 Feb: Simple Minds – Belfast Child;	2 weeks
11 Mar: Jason Donovan – Too Many Broken Hearts;	2 weeks
25 Mar: Madonna – Like A Prayer;	3 weeks
15 Apr: The Bangles – Eternal Flame;	4 weeks
13 May: Kylie Minogue – Hand On Your Heart;	1 week
20 May: Gerry Marsden/Paul McCartney/Holly Johnson/Christians –	
Ferry 'Cross The Mersey;	3 weeks
10 Jun: Jason Donovan – Sealed With A Kiss;	2 weeks
24 Jun: Soul II Soul featuring Caron Wheeler – Back To Life;	4 weeks
22 Jul: Sonia – You'll Never Stop Me Loving You;	2 weeks
05 Aug: Jive Bunny & The Mastermixers – Swing The Mood;	5 weeks
09 Sep: Black Box – Ride On Time;	6 weeks
21 Oct: Jive Bunny & The Mastermixers – That's What I Like;	3 weeks
11 Nov: Lisa Stansfield – All Around The World;	2 weeks
25 Nov: The New Kids On The Block – You Got It (The Right Stuff);	3 weeks
16 Dec: Jive Bunny & The Mastermixers – Let's Party;	1 week
23 Dec: Band Aid II – Do They Know It's Christmas;	2 weeks

THE US NUMBER ONE SINGLES OF 1989

07 Jan: Poison – Every Rose Has Its Thorn;	1 week
14 Jan: Bobby Brown – My Prerogative;	1 week
21 Jan: Phil Collins – Two Hearts;	2 weeks
04 Feb: Sheriff – When I'm With You;	1 week
11 Feb: Paula Abdul – Straight Up;	3 weeks
04 Mar: Debbie Gibson – Lost In Your Eyes;	3 weeks
25 Mar: Mike & The Mechanics – The Living Years;	1 week
01 Apr: The Bangles – Eternal Flame;	1 week
08 Apr: Roxette – The Look;	1 week
15 Apr: Fine Young Cannibals – She Drives Me Crazy;	1 week
22 Apr: Madonna – Like A Prayer;	3 weeks
13 May: Bon Jovi – I'll Be There For You;	1 week
20 May: Paula Abdul – Forever Your Girl;	2 weeks
03 Jun: Michael Damian – Rock On;	1 week
10 Jun: Bette Midler – Wind Beneath My Wings;	1 week
17 Jun: The New Kids On The Block – I'll Be Loving You (Forever);	1 week
24 Jun: Richard Marx – Satisfied;	1 week
01 Jul: Milli Vanilli – Baby Don't Forget My Number;	1 week
08 Jul: Fine Young Cannibals – Good Thing;	1 week
15 Jul: Simply Red – If You Don't Know Me By Now;	1 week
22 Jul: Martika – Toy Soldiers;	2 weeks
05 Aug: Prince – Batdance;	1 week
12 Aug: Richard Marx – Right Here Waiting;	3 weeks
02 Sep: Paula Abdul – Cold Hearted;	1 week
09 Sep: The New Kids On The Block – Hangin' Tough;	1 week
16 Sep: Gloria Estefan – Don't Wanna Lose You;	1 week
23 Sep: Milli Vanilli – Girl I'm Gonna Miss You;	2 weeks
07 Oct: Janet Jackson – Miss You Much;	4 weeks
04 Nov: Roxette – Listen To Your Heart;	1 week
11 Nov: Bad English – When I See You Smile;	2 weeks
25 Nov: Milli Vanilli – Blame It On The Rain;	2 weeks
09 Dec: Billy Joel – We Didn't Start The Fire;	2 weeks
23 Dec: Phil Collins – Another Day In Paradise;	2 weeks

THE 'UNSUCCESSFUL' UK NUMBER
TWO SINGLES OF 1989

07 Jan: Erasure – Crackers International E.P.;	3 weeks
28 Jan: Mike & The Mechanics – The Living Years;	3 weeks
25 Feb: Michael Ball – Love Changes Everything;	2 weeks
04 Mar: Michael Jackson – Leave Me Alone;	1 week
15 Apr: Simply Red – If You Don't Know Me By Now;	3 weeks
03 Jun: Natalie Cole – Miss You Like Crazy;	1 week
10 Jun: Cliff Richard – The Best Of Me;	2 weeks
01 Jul: Prince – Batdance;	1 week
08 Jul: The Beautiful South – Song For Whoever;	1 week
22 Jul: London Boys – London Nights;	1 week
29 Jul: Bros – Too Much;	1 week
05 Aug: Kylie Minogue – Wouldn't Change A Thing;	2 weeks
19 Aug: Lil' Louis – French Kiss;	1 week
26 Aug: Alice Cooper – Poison;	1 week
16 Sep: Jason Donovan – Every Day I Love You More;	1 week
23 Sep: Richard Marx – Right Here Waiting;	2 weeks
07 Oct: Technotronic Featuring Felly – Pump Up The Jam;	2 weeks
28 Oct: Milli Vanilli – Girl I'm Gonna Miss You;	3 weeks
18 Nov: Phil Collins – Another Day In Paradise;	1 week
02 Dec: Linda Ronstadt & Aaron Neville – Don't Know Much;	2 weeks
16 Dec: Jason Donovan – When You Come Back To Me;	3 weeks

THE 'UNSUCCESSFUL' US NUMBER TWO SINGLES OF 1989

21 Jan: Taylor Dayne – Don't Rush Me

18 Feb: Tone Loc – Wild Thing

04 Mar: Sheena Easton – Lover In Me

01 Apr: Milli Vanilli – Girl You Know It's True

20 May: Jody Watley – Real Love

03 Jun: Donny Osmond – Soldier Of Love

15 Jul: Madonna – Express Yourself

05 Aug: Bobby Brown – On Your Own

23 Sep: Warrant – Heaven

07 Oct: Madonna – Cherish

21 Oct: The Cure – Love Song

28 Oct: Tears For Fears – Sowing The Seeds Of Love

04 Nov: The New Kids On The Block – Cover Girl

23 Dec: Linda Ronstadt & Aaron Neville – Don't Know Much

NEWS HIGHLIGHTS OF 1989

January 8th: A passenger aeroplane crashes in the east Midlands.

January 14th: 'The Satanic Verses' are publicly burnt in Bradford.

January 20th: George Bush is sworn in as the American President.

February 12th: Belfast solicitor Pat Finucane is shot dead.

February 14th: Salman Rushdie is 'sentenced to death' by Iran.

February 25th: Mike Tyson defeats Frank Bruno in a boxing fight.

March 4th: Five people die in a rail crash at Purley.

March 15th: A rally in Budapest demands democracy and reform.

March 24th: The Exxon Valdez causes a huge oil spillage in Alaska.

April 7th: Mikhail Gorbachev meets the Queen at Windsor Castle.

April 15th: Almost 100 football fans are crushed at Hillsborough.

April 17th: An eight–year ban on Solidarity is lifted in Poland.

May 15th: Carlos Menem wins the Argentine presidential election.

May 17th: Vaclav Havel is freed from prison in Prague.

May 19th: Inflation in Britain rises to eight per cent.

June 8th: Britain votes in the latest European parliament elections.

June 19th: Solidarity triumphs at the Polish senate elections.

June 29th: Charles Haughey resigns as the Irish Prime Minister.

July 5th: President Botha pays a visit to Nelson Mandela.

July 5th: Oliver North is given a suspended jail term.

July 15th: The British Lions achieve a series win in Australia.

August 1st: Australia regain the Ashes against a hapless England.

August 14th: President Botha of South Africa resigns.

August 14th: The West Midlands serious crimes squad is disbanded.

September 11th: Hungary opens its border with Austria.

September 22nd: An IRA bomb kills ten Royal Marines.

September 26th: The last Vietnamese troops leave Cambodia.

October 11th: England qualify for the 1990 World Cup finals.

October 19th: The convicted Guildford Four are released from jail.

October 26th: Nigel Lawson resigns as Chancellor of the Exchequer.

November 10th: The Berlin Wall is dismantled and surmounted.

November 15th: Scotland qualify for the 1990 World Cup finals.

November 21st: The House of Commons is finally televised.

December 6th: Egon Krenz is deposed as the East German leader.

December 10th: The Dalai Lama is awarded the Nobel Peace Prize.

December 29th: Vaclav Havel becomes Czechoslovakia's President.

SPORT IN 1989

English Division One football champions: Arsenal; runners–up: Liverpool

English FA Cup final: Liverpool 3 Everton 2 (after extra time)

English League Cup Final: Nottingham Forest 3 Luton Town 1

Scottish Premier League football champions: Glasgow Rangers; runners–up: Aberdeen

Scottish FA Cup final: Glasgow Celtic 1 Glasgow Rangers 0

Scottish League Cup final: Glasgow Rangers 3 Aberdeen 2

Irish League football champions: Linfield; Irish Cup final: Ballymena United 1 Larne 0

League Of Ireland football champions: Waterford; cup winners: Bohemians

European Cup final: AC Milan 4 Steaua Bucuresti 0

European Cup–Winners' Cup final: Barcelona 2 Sampdoria 0

UEFA Cup final: Napoli beat VfB Stuttgart 5–4 on aggregate

English county cricket champions: Worcestershire

Five Nations' rugby union champions: France (6 points)

Formula One world drivers' champion: Alain Prost (France) in a McLaren car

Gaelic football All–Ireland champions: Cork; runners–up: Mayo

British Open golf champion: Mark Calcavecchia (at Royal Troon)

US Masters golf champion: Nick Faldo

US Open golf champion: Curtis Strange

USPGA golf champion: Payne Stewart

Rugby league Challenge Cup final: Wigan 27 St Helens 0

Wimbledon men's singles tennis final: B Becker beat S Edberg 6–0, 7–6, 6–4

Wimbledon ladies' singles tennis final: S Graf beat M Navratilova 6–2, 6–7, 6–1

World snooker final: Steve Davis (England) beat John Parrott (England) 18–3

The Aintree Grand National steeplechase winner: Little Polveir; price 28–1

The Epsom Derby winner: Nashwan; jockey – Willie Carson; price 5–4F

The Ryder Cup: Europe 14 The United States Of America 14

1989's BUCKET-KICKERS

January 7th: Emperor Hirohito of Japan; aged 87

January 23rd: Salvador Dali (Spanish artist); aged 84

January 27th: Thomas Sopwith (ex–British pilot); aged 101

February 2nd: Sir William Stephenson (British spy); aged 93

February 17th: Guy Laroche (French couturier); aged 67

February 27th: Konrad Zacharias Lorenz (Austrian zoologist); aged 85

March 14th: Zita of Austria (ex–Empress); aged 96

April 12th: Sugar Ray Robinson (US boxer); aged 67

April 15th: Hu Yaobang (Chinese politician); aged 73

April 19th: Daphne du Maurier (British novelist); aged 81

April 26th: Lucille Ball (US comedienne); aged 77

June 4th: Ruhollah Musavi Khomeini (Iranian leader); aged 86

June 27th: A.J. Ayer (British philosopher); aged 78

July 2nd: Andrei Gromyko (Soviet statesman); aged 79

July 6th: Janos Kadar (Hungarian leader); aged 77

July 11th: Lord Laurence Olivier (British actor); aged 82

July 16th: Herbert von Karajan (Austrian conductor); aged 70

August 21st: George Adamson (Kenyan conservationist); aged 83

August 23rd: R.D. Laing (British psychiatrist); aged 61

August 24th: Feliks Topolski (British artist); aged 82

August 29th: Sir Peter Scott (British naturalist); aged 79

September 4th: Georges Simenon (Belgian novelist); aged 86

September 22nd: Irving Berlin (US songwriter); aged 101

September 28th: Ferdinand Marcos (ex–Filipino leader); aged 72

October 6th: Bette Davis (US actress); aged 81

October 20th: Sir Anthony Quayle (British actor); aged 76

November 5th: Vladimir Horowitz (Russian pianist); aged 85

November 12th: Dolores Ibarruri Gomez (Spanish politician); aged 93

November 22nd: Rene Moawad (Lebanon's President); aged 64

December 14th: Andrei Sakharov (Soviet physicist); aged 68

December 22nd: Samuel Beckett (Irish writer); aged 83

December 25th: Nicolae Ceausescu (Rumanian dictator); aged 71

APPENDIX I
THE TOP TEN BIGGEST-SELLING
UK SINGLES OF THE 1980s

1 Do They Know It's Christmas by Band Aid (1984)

2 Relax by Frankie Goes To Hollywood (1984)

3 I Just Called To Say I Love You by Stevie Wonder (1984)

4 Two Tribes by Frankie Goes To Hollywood (1984)

5 Don't You Want Me by Human League (1981)

6 Last Christmas/Everything She Wants by Wham! (1984)

7 Karma Chameleon by Culture Club (1983)

8 Careless Whisper by George Michael (1984)

9 The Power Of Love by Jennifer Rush (1985)

10 Come On Eileen by Dexy's Midnight Runners (1982)

APPENDIX II
25 GREAT INSTRUMENTALS
OF THE 1980s

Adella by UB40 (1980)

Axel F by Harold Faltermeyer (1984)

Chariots Of Fire by Vangelis (1981)

Close To The Edit by Art Of Noise (1984)

Crockett's Theme by Jan Hammer (1987)

Droned by Phil Collins (1981)

Easter Island by Rico (1982)

Elegia by New Order (1985)

Europa by Blondie (1980)

Exodus by Bad Manners (1982)

4th of July by U2 (1984)

Go For It by Stiff Little Fingers (1981)

Holiday Fortnight by The Specials (1980)

Mantovani by The Swinging Cats (1980)

On A Train by The Cure (1980)

Oscillate Wildly by The Smiths (1985)

Riot City by Jerry Dammers (1986)

Somebody Up There Likes You by Simple Minds (1982)

Space Invaders by The Pretenders (1980)

The Longships by Enya (1988)

The Opium Eaters by Madness (1981)

The Teams That Meet In Caffs by Dexys Midnight Runners (1980)

The Wild Cats Of Kilkenny by The Pogues (1985)

Time Is Tight by The Clash (1980)

Zaar by Peter Gabriel (1988)

APPENDIX III
30 MORE RECOMMENDED ALBUMS
OF THE 1980s

Searching For The Young Soul Rebels by Dexy's Midnight Runners (1980)

Sound Affects by The Jam (1980)

Uprising by Bob Marley And The Wailers (1980)

Face Value by Phil Collins (1981)

Wha'appen by The Beat (1981)

Pretenders II by The Pretenders (1981)

The Hunter by Blondie (1982)

Combat Rock by The Clash (1982)

The Nightfly by Donald Fagen (1982)

Colour By Numbers by Culture Club (1983)

She Bop by Cyndi Lauper (1983)

The Final Cut by Pink Floyd (1983)

Keep Moving by Madness (1984)

Hatful Of Hollow by The Smiths (1984)

In The Studio by The Special AKA (1984)

Rum, Sodomy, And The Lash by The Pogues (1985)

Raindogs by Tom Waits (1985)

The Secret Of Association by Paul Young (1985)

A Different Light by The Bangles (1986)

So by Peter Gabriel (1986)

A Kind Of Magic by Queen (1986)

Sign 'O' The Times by Prince (1987)

Bad by Michael Jackson (1987)

Actually by The Pet Shop Boys (1987)

Bummed by The Happy Mondays (1988)

Green by R.E.M. (1988)

Fisherman's Blues by The Waterboys (1988)

Like A Prayer by Madonna (1989)

Technique by New Order (1989)

Bleach by Nirvana (1989)

APPENDIX IV
GONE, BUT NOT FORGOTTEN

Here are thirty more tracks from the 1980s which are worthy of special mention:

Together We Are Beautiful by Fern Kinney (1980)

Echo Beach by Martha And The Muffins (1980)

Too Experienced by The Bodysnatchers (1980)

Xanadu by Olivia Newton–John And E.L.O. (1980)

It's Only Love by Elvis Presley (1980)

One Day I'll Fly Away by Randy Crawford (1980)

Fade To Grey by Visage (1980)

Dancing On The Floor (Hooked On Love) by Third World (1981)

Centerfold by J.Geils Band (1982)

Steppin' Out by Joe Jackson (1983)

The Price Of Admission by Stiff Little Fingers (1983)

Cruel Summer by Bananarama (1983)

Smalltown Boy by Bronski Beat (1984)

Drive by The Cars (1984)

No More Lonely Nights by Paul McCartney (1984)

Brothers In Arms by Dire Straits (1985)

Downtown Train by Tom Waits (1985)

Nikita by Elton John (1985)

On My Own by Patti LaBelle And Michael MacDonald (1986)

Rodrigo Bay by Working Week (1986)

Stuck With You by Huey Lewis And The News (1986)

Take My Breath Away by Berlin (1986)

Mary's Prayer by Danny Wilson (1987)

Somewhere In My Heart by Aztec Camera (1988)

Tribute (Right On) by The Pasadenas (1988)

I Don't Want To Talk About It by Everything But The Girl (1988)

Mad Cyril by The Happy Mondays (1988)

Rush Hour by Jane Wiedlin (1988)

The First Time by Robin Beck (1988)

You're History by Shakespear's Sister (1989)

APPENDIX V
THE OSCAR WINNERS OF THE 1980s

1980: BEST PICTURE – Ordinary People (directed by Robert Redford)

1980: BEST ACTOR – Robert De Niro (Raging Bull)

1980: BEST ACTRESS – Sissy Spacek (Coal Miner's Daughter)

1981: BEST PICTURE – Chariots Of Fire (directed by Hugh Hudson)

1981: BEST ACTOR – Henry Fonda (On Golden Pond)

1981: BEST ACTRESS – Katharine Hepburn (On Golden Pond)

1982: BEST PICTURE – Gandhi (directed by Richard Attenborough)

1982: BEST ACTOR – Ben Kingsley (Gandhi)

1982: BEST ACTRESS – Meryl Streep (Sophie's Choice)

1983: BEST PICTURE – Terms Of Endearment (directed by James L. Brooks)

1983: BEST ACTOR – Robert Duvall (Tender Mercies)

1983: BEST ACTRESS – Shirley Maclaine (Terms Of Endearment)

1984: BEST PICTURE – Amadeus (directed by Milos Forman)

1984: BEST ACTOR – F. Murray Abraham (Amadeus)

1984: BEST ACTRESS – Sally Field (Places In The Heart)

1985: BEST PICTURE – Out Of Africa (directed by Sydney Pollack)

1985: BEST ACTOR – William Hurt (Kiss Of The Spider Woman)

1985: BEST ACTRESS – Geraldine Page (The Trip To Bountiful)

1986: BEST PICTURE – Platoon (directed by Oliver Stone)

1986: BEST ACTOR – Paul Newman (The Color Of Money)

1986: BEST ACTRESS – Marlee Matlin (Children Of A Lesser God)

1987: BEST PICTURE – The Last Emperor (directed by Bernardo Bertolucci)

1987: BEST ACTOR – Michael Douglas (Wall Street)

1987: BEST ACTRESS – Cher (Moonstruck)

1988: BEST PICTURE – Rain Man (directed by Barry Levinson)

1988: BEST ACTOR – Dustin Hoffman (Rain Man)

1988: BEST ACTRESS – Jodie Foster (The Accused)

1989: BEST PICTURE – Driving Miss Daisy (directed by Bruce Beresford)

1989: BEST ACTOR – Daniel Day–Lewis (My Left Foot)

1989: BEST ACTRESS – Jessica Tandy (Driving Miss Daisy)

About the Publishers

If you are desperately trying to get a foot in the door and get your book into the public domain, you could do worse than submit a sample of it to ourselves, preferably on a disc and/or in PDF format. We are Parkbench Publications, PO Box 1081, Belfast, BT1 9EP. Unlike most publishers, we will not put your sample to the bottom of a pile and then glance at it several weeks later. You will receive a quick decision and your project will be afforded the respect that it deserves, which is uncommon amongst the major publishing houses that will not entertain you unless you have a cookery programme on Channel Four or appear regularly in OK magazine.

Alternatively, you can waste time circulating samples to the major publishing houses and wait literally months for their standard, tiresome 'good luck elsewhere' replies.

ABBA BEATLES BOWIE CREAM DOORS ELVIS FREE HENDRIX MADONNA MARLEY ZEPPELIN WHO U2 UB40 STONES REM

THE SONG FOR TODAY

by Jimmie Oliver

(featuring 366 songs:
1 for each day of the year)

Parkbench Publications

NIRVANA OASIS PRINCE QUEEN

This excellent reference book features songs from such artists as: the Beach Boys/the Beat/the Bonzo Dog Doo Dah Band/Kate Bush/the Byrds/Eric Clapton/the Clash/ Culture Club/Depeche Mode/Duran Duran/the Eagles/Marvin Gaye/the Happy Mondays/Iron Maiden/the Jam/Jethro Tull/John Lennon/Madness/the Mamas And The Papas/Manfred Mann/Massive Attack/the Moody Blues/New Order/Nilsson/ Roy Orbison/the Pet Shop Boys/Pink Floyd/the Pretenders/Public Image Limited/ Diana Ross/the Sex Pistols/Simple Minds/Slade/the Small Faces/the Specials/Status Quo/Rod Stewart/the Stone Roses/the Supremes/T Rex/Talking Heads/the Three Degrees/Ike And Tina Turner/the Velvet Underground/Neil Young/Paul Young/ Wings ... and lots more!

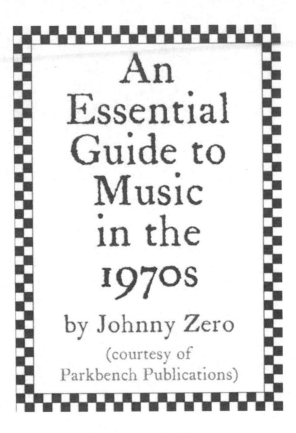

An Essential Guide to Music in the 1970s

by Johnny Zero

(courtesy of Parkbench Publications)

This 360-page well of information contains the following:

Every Top 10 UK singles chart in the 1970s

The Number 1 UK album for each week

The Number 1 US album for each week

The Number 1 US single for each week

A top news story for each week

The concert highlights of each year

The sporting highlights of each year

The deaths of each year

The Oscar winners of the 1970s

Plus extra coverage of 120 notable recordings

Featured albums from Led Zeppelin, the Rolling Stones, Neil Young, Elton John, Bob Marley And The Wailers, Pink Floyd, the Eagles, Fleetwood Mac, Kate Bush, and Blondie